THE FAMILY
BUSINESS
BLUEPRINT

THE FAMILY
BUSINESS
BLUEPRINT

Creating Your Succession Roadmap
- How To Maximize Your Exit, Setting Yourself
And The Next Generation Up For Success

CHUCK COOPER

CONTENTS

FOREWORD

by Dr. Joey Faucette
Positive Culture Architect, best-selling author,
and host of the Work Positive Podcast.
https://workpositive.today

You live long enough, and it all starts to shift.

Sure, your chest shifts down. The cumulative effect of gravity, right?

But it's more than that.

Other gravities weigh you down, too.

Your mindset pulls you down and shifts from infinite to finite: "I don't have as long to do what I want to do."

Your perspective pushes you down and shifts from today to tomorrow: "What legacy will I leave my children?"

Your reality shifts polarities from what is to what could be: "What will my employees do to provide for their families if my kids don't want this business and it closes?"

There's no fighting gravity.

However, you can escape it long enough to leverage it.

Now it takes a great deal of fuel. Watch the multiple SpaceX launches. The intense burning of fuel in a contained explosion lifts the payloads higher and higher until it escapes gravity. Ninety percent of the rocket's fuel burns in those initial stages.

The goal is for the payload to establish its own path.

If it's a Starlink satellite, the goal is a low orbit. Leverage Earth's gravity and create a high enough arc to avoid crashing and burning through the atmosphere and yet low enough to provide an Internet signal to rooftop dishes.

What kind of path does your business have?

An orbit that's high enough to leverage all of the sweat equity you poured into it?

And yet low enough to avoid crashing and burning without you but continue the heart and soul of your legacy?

Like you, I own a business. A few of them, in fact.

But I'm no rocket scientist.

I need help figuring out the calculus to escape the gravity of the grind. Calculating how much fuel I need to get off the launchpad of creating a succession plan. Deciphering if my payload delivery could or even should include family members.

I need a flight plan destined to deliver

I bet you do, too.

Chuck Cooper is my rocket scientist. He's my engineer who guides the intense calculations of what I need to do to get my company ready, where I best fly it and who are the most gifted pilots in steering as I leave the capsule.

This book is Chuck's gift to us. He distills the complex calculations of family business into language we can understand as business owners confronting our own shifts.

Read every word of this book.

Highlight it.

Talk about it with your leadership team, family members, and others like you facing the shift.

Then start your countdown with Chuck seated next to you.

Here's to the successful delivery of your legacy company to the next generation.

INTRODUCTION

Legacy's Burden

Have you ever felt the weight of your ambitions, your dreams, pressing down on you like an invisible burden?

Have you ever poured your heart and soul into something, only to wonder what will become of it once you're no longer there to tend to it?

If so, then the story of Joe Davis and Davis Manufacturing may resonate deeply with you.

In the heart of a bustling Midwest town, amid the streets where dreams met reality, stood Davis Manufacturing—a testament to one person's unwavering determination. For over three decades, Joe Davis poured his soul into every aspect of the company. It wasn't just a business; it was his life's work, his legacy, his identity. Perhaps you, too, have invested yourself wholly in a pursuit, be it a career, a project, or a cause.

Joe's journey, from humble beginnings in a small garage to a sprawling complex that employed what seemed like half the town, is the stuff of local legend. His story speaks of the power of perseverance, hard work, and a relentless pursuit of one's goals. But amidst the accolades and success, there lay a hidden burden—a fear of what would become of his legacy once he hung up his boots.

His children, Ben and Julie, had never known a life beyond the shadow of the factory's smokestacks. Like Joe, you may have silent hopes for the future, dreams of passing on your legacy to the next generation. Yet, like Joe, you may also grapple with the fear of voicing these expectations, fearing rejection or indifference.

As the years pass, it's easy to become trapped in a cycle of uncertainty, unable to envision a life beyond the walls of your own empire. Perhaps retirement seems like a distant fantasy, overshadowed by the demands of the present. But what if fate, in its unpredictable nature, forces you to confront the stark reality of your mortality?

After years of putting off succession planning, Joe had a sudden health scare that forced him to take action.

Feeling overly tired, Joe told his wife he was going to bed early that evening, and when he woke the next morning, he had developed stroke-like symptoms, leaving him unable to walk and with blurred vision.

Joe recovered and returned to his normal routine. However, he continued to ignore the need for a proactive succession plan. Today, the buildings that once housed a thriving business sit empty and lifeless, serving only as a memory for those who live in that small town.

This event serves as a poignant reminder of the fragility of life and the fleeting success of our achievements. It compels us to ask ourselves: what will become of our life's work once we're no longer able to tend to it? Will it fade into obscurity, or will we entrust it to another's hands, uncertain of what tomorrow might bring?

In the twilight of his years, Joe Davis stood at the crossroads of past and future, grappling with the legacy he'd built and the legacy yet to be written. And as the sun set on Davis Manufacturing, only time would tell what tomorrow held for the dreams of yesterday. But his story isn't just his own—it's a reflection of our own struggles, our own fears, our own hopes for the future.

It's truly inspiring to hear about entrepreneurs like you, who have dedicated so much of themselves—time, energy, and financial resources—into building something genuinely remarkable. Reflecting on the journey, it's clear how much pride and fulfillment come from seeing your vision come to life, impacting not just your life, but also the lives of your family, friends, and the wider community. The bonds formed with customers, the opportunities provided to others, and the legacy built within the community are truly invaluable.

However, a crucial question looms:

What happens to this labor of love, your business, when you're no longer at the helm?

Like many of you, I've faced similar contemplations. Starting my own financial services business taught me a vital lesson about the importance of planning for the future, especially when it involves difficult conversations about our mortality. It's not an easy topic; our clients did not want to think or talk about it until a third party sat with them and facilitated the meetings. It was an important step, as it was the bridge that led to developing and executing plans which brought multiple generations of a family together.

This challenge isn't unique to individuals; it's remarkably prevalent among small and midsize business owners, too. Our research shows that as of December 2023, there were 33,185,550 small businesses[1] in the United States, according to the Small Business Administration. And yet, more than 23,000,000 business owners have no formal succession plan.

You may be asking, "what is the impact of not having a succession plan?" Studies from the Small Business Administration consistently document less than 30% of small businesses transition to the 2nd generation, 12% to the 3rd generation and only 3% to the 4th generation.[2]

---

[1] https://advocacy.sba.gov/
[2] SBA

Yet, today, 40% of small businesses in the United States[3] are owned by someone in the Baby Boomer generation, meaning even the youngest of these is 60 years of age. With an overwhelming number of businesses lacking a formal succession plan, the urgency becomes even more pronounced as we approach a significant period of transition for Baby Boomer and GenX-owned businesses. The statistics are stark, yet they highlight a crucial opportunity for preparedness and foresight.

Imagine your business, your passion, struggling to exist beyond your time. The stark reality? Less than 30% of businesses make it to the second generation. This isn't just about numbers; it's about your legacy, your family's future.

The hurdles—fear, uncertainty, a perceived lack of time—can seem insurmountable. Yet, this calls for a profound shift in perspective. It's time to view succession planning not as a daunting task but as an act of love and commitment to your family's security and legacy. Embrace it with determination. Your business is a *legacy* that will inspire and benefit generations to come. Let this realization fuel your action to secure the future.

The succession planning process should start early in the business's life or as soon as possible under your leadership, realizing that succession planning is a present-day business strategy and not an end-of-life task. Achieving generational success involves investment in both the business and family relationships to maintain continuity and readiness for growth.

---

3 https://guidantfinancial.com

Whether you run a family-owned business or a small or medium-sized enterprise without family involvement, this book is for you. Throughout our research, we spoke with a diverse group of business owners, from those managing multi-generational family businesses to those leading partnerships or managing roles in non-family firms. Despite these differences, we found that all of you face similar challenges and risks. This book is designed to address these shared issues and provide valuable insights to help all small and midsize business owners succeed.

This book aims to empower you with clear insights into four crucial aspects, enabling you to make more informed decisions. These include:

1. Understanding the purpose of a succession plan and its importance
2. Essentials for your succession plan and assembling your ideal team
3. Exploring options for choosing a successor
4. Leveraging resources to enhance your company's value, personal transition, and financial plan

As Jack Canfield said, "Everything you want is on the other side of fear." Know this, you are not alone. Let's embark on this journey together, securing your business and a meaningful legacy for the generations to come.

READER'S TESTIMONIALS

As an owner of a small business that does work that matters, I want to make sure the entity can have multi-generational success and impact. Thank you, Chuck, for creating a resource to help me navigate toward leaving that kind of legacy.

– Bob Borcherdt; Founder and CEO of IN2GREAT

The Family Business Blueprint is going to change lives! This book is an invaluable resource for business owners and their families, helping them to plan for and navigate challenges that arise as older generations are looking to retire. The tools in this book will provide you a roadmap to success so that you can avoid common pitfalls and set yourself up for success!

– Lo Myrick, Mindset Coach & Consultant

In The Family Business Blueprint: Creating Your Succession Roadmap, Chuck masterfully combines his deep experience, his many interviews with business owners, and his passion to create a clear roadmap and guide to succession planning. This is a must-read for every owner and senior leader of a family-owned business!

– Doug Havas; Founder & President Pinnacle Sales Advisors

An essential read for any family business owner, Chuck draws on his deep experience to expertly navigate the complexities of planning a successful exit and explores all succession planning options with clarity and insight. It's a comprehensive guide that transforms a daunting process into a manageable and strategic journey.

– Paul Wehrly; Founder & President Sage Sales Advisors

Feeling overwhelmed by the uncertainty of your business's future without you? Chuck provides a comprehensive roadmap to master succession planning, ensuring your hard-earned legacy thrives for years to come. This is essential reading for anyone trying to secure their life's work, leave an inspiring legacy for generations, or watch their dreams flourish beyond their wildest expectations!

– Nick Whitney; EOS Implementer and Author of The Beaver's Blueprint: Escaping the Hamster Wheel to Achieve Your Dam Goals

Succession planning is something every business owner NEEDS to do, but far too many wait until it's too late before the delay creates a mess. Navigating this terrain requires a proven guide who knows this mountain well. Family-owned businesses require even more expertise, as family dynamics can make succession planning dicey. The Family Business Blueprint is an excellent resource that every family-owned business leader needs to read.

– Gary Frey; Author, Silence The Imposter: 7 Weapons To Silence Imposter Syndrome

In "The Family Business Blueprint: Creating Your Succession Roadmap", Chuck Cooper provides invaluable insights and actionable recommendations for business owners and their key stakeholders. Emphasizing planning, purpose, meaning and joy, he sets the stage for a successful present and a fulfilling future. Remember to be intentional about your future, take action, and make informed decisions. Enjoy the journey!"

– Tim N. Turrittin; Founder & Sr. Partner, One Domino

I highly recommend The Family Business Blueprint. This book is a game-changer for family-owned enterprises. Its actionable advice and thorough approach make it an indispensable resource for building a lasting legacy. Every page is filled with practical insights and strategies that will guide family businesses toward sustainable success and harmony. If you are committed to ensuring the longevity and prosperity of your family enterprise, "The Family Business Blueprint" is a must-read.

– Bob Gors; President, BLU -Business Leaders Unleashed

The Family Business Blueprint should be required reading for business owners. The author underscores the importance of a systematic, well-structured succession plan and provides a strategic roadmap to ensure an effective legacy transition.

– Ken Myers; Regional Sales Manager, Coadvantage

It's a fact: all business owners will eventually exit their companies -- under their own power or being wheeled away on a stretcher. If you're not planning to die at your desk, this book is for you.

The Family Business Blueprint: Creating Your Succession Roadmap is an important guide to the processes and pitfalls found in any business transition. Chuck Cooper has managed to pack a great deal of analysis into an easy-to-read manual for business owners who are looking to pass the keys to a new owner -- family, employees, or buyer. He explores all these options and has advice that will make any transition smoother. When you're ready to plan your exit, you couldn't ask for a better starting point than to read this book.

> **– David Worrell, Founder / CFO, FuseCFO, and author of "The Entrepreneurs Guide to Financial Statements"**

CHAPTER 1

There's No Buyer for Your Baby

In 2022, following the release of my book *Unprecedented*, I found myself in the midst of a pivotal moment at Georgetown University. Invited to speak to a group of ambitious international students immersed in an entrepreneurship intensive, little did I anticipate the profound impact that one question would have on both me and the trajectory of my work.

Among the sea of eager faces, one question resonated with a large number of the students:

"My parents own a very successful business, and there is an unspoken expectation that my career will be spent running the company. However, I do not want to be involved in the family business. How do I navigate this conversation with them, expressing my alternative ambitions?"

It was this question, teeming with complexity and personal conflict, that ignited the spark for what would become the foundation of this book.

The genesis of this journey, however, extends far beyond that singular moment. Over the past year, my team and I invested a significant amount of time speaking with and interviewing small and midsize businesses across the United States. We uncovered an important truth while engaging in candid conversations with over 1,000 business owners and another 350 next gen leaders: The failure to create a detailed succession plan threatens the downfall of small businesses across the United States, and in turn, threatens their families and communities.

As we talked with the business owners, we began to recognize some key differences in the mindset and management priorities between owners who had implemented a succession plan versus those who had not, and the differences were telling.

In many cases, owners who had implemented succession plans spoke about revenue growth, best practices, operational excellence, talent development, and company culture. These owners had a vision, and although they had to adapt along the way, they were engaged and optimistic about their future. These owners were not only willing to invest in themselves with business coaches or memberships within peer groups—like Vistage, C12, EO, and Convene—but they were also focused on developing their people through leadership training and mentoring programs. These forward-thinking business owners understood the importance of using technology and having systems and processes in place so the entire organization would thrive without them.

On the other hand, owners who had not done succession planning were not as confident, often unsure in how they would handle unexpected events. They were consumed with battling talent acquisition, retention issues, and day-to-day operations. In many cases, everything, including sales, service, marketing, operations, and vendor relationships, flowed through their office. Ultimately, they became the bottleneck within their own company, which prevented client acquisition and revenue growth while increasing risk for client loss.

One business owner we spoke with in Arizona shared his story: he spent years ensuring the progress and growth for his company first-hand, until one day, he went to have his annual physical, and a series of tests led to a diagnosis with surgical correction. He was forced to leave work for a minimum of four to six months.

It was at this point he realized the consequences of having a reactive management style—and the consequences of failing to put a succession plan in place.

A good team can hold everything together in your absence; with a great team, you can continue to grow the business hands-free.

However, with a below average operation, you could be looking at tens of thousands, even hundreds of thousands, in losses the moment you're absent.

Bottom line, succession planning is a necessity. Most business owners, especially those of small and midsize family businesses, recognize this fact. But the complexity of their roles and the sheer volume of time the day-to-day tasks require often sideline critical long-term planning efforts. The intricate dance between managing daily operations and carving out space for strategic planning, like succession planning, is fraught with challenges.

Here's a deeper look at six of the most common responses we heard when discussing barriers for succession planning:

1. Perceived Complexity and Time Consumption

Operating a business means maneuvering through a complex array of tasks, choices, and obligations. This setting generates significant complexity, especially as you tackle the various layers of your business activities. When it comes to strategic planning, such as succession planning, the complexity intensifies.

Succession planning is not merely about choosing a successor; it involves preparing the business for a smooth transition, ensuring financial stability, and considering the emotional and psychological impacts on all stakeholders. The complexity of these considerations can make starting the process seem daunting, especially when daily operations already demand so much attention.

Time is a finite resource, and for small business owners, it's often in short supply. The bulk of your days are consumed by immediate operational needs—solving problems, making sales, managing staff—which leaves little room for the deep, focused thought required for effective strategic planning.

Succession planning, for instance, is a process that can't be rushed; it requires thoughtful consideration of many factors, including the future direction of the business, the abilities of potential successors, and the legal and financial frameworks needed to support the transition. Given the urgent demands of the present, finding time for these long-term considerations can feel next to impossible.

The consequences of this tension between immediate demands and the need for strategic planning can be profound. Without a clear succession plan, a business is vulnerable to instability in the event of your sudden departure, whether due to retirement, illness, or other unforeseen circumstances. The lack of such planning jeopardizes the legacy of the business, its financial health, and the livelihoods of employees and other stakeholders.

To mitigate these risks and ensure a future for the business beyond your tenure, you must find ways to address the challenges of perceived complexity and time consumption.

2. Uncertainty about the Future

As a family business owner, uncertainty is everywhere. Market volatility, rising costs, shrinking margins, and events like COVID-19 make it tough to chart a clear path for your business. Concerns about altering your business's legacy, family dynamics, and financial worries further complicate decision-making.

Economic shifts, higher interest rates, inflation, technological advancements, and changing consumer behaviors create an unpredictable environment, making succession planning feel overwhelming. On a personal level, your business represents years of dreams and hard work. Handing over control can feel like giving up a piece of yourself, and family dynamics add complexity. Balancing different aspirations and maintaining harmony can be challenging, leading to worries about conflicts and support for your chosen successor.

Political instability affects market conditions and regulations, adding to the uncertainty. Struggling to attract and retain talent further complicates succession planning, making you question if your business will have the necessary resources and leadership to thrive. Constant changes in economic trends, technology, and global events lead to hesitation and a lack of confidence in making long-term plans.

The fear of the succession planning process and potential changes can be daunting, making the thought of diving into a complex, disruptive process intimidating. These factors create significant barriers to succession planning.

However, *acknowledging these fears is the first step to overcoming them*. By addressing these uncertainties head-on, you can move forward with a plan that secures both your legacy and your business's future.

Succession planning isn't about letting go; it's about ensuring your hard work endures, honoring your legacy, and paving the way for future generations.

---

3. Emotional Attachment

The deep emotional attachment you feel toward your business is seen as an extension of yourself, intertwining your personal identity with that of your company. This connection makes the idea of succession planning—a stark acknowledgment of a future without your day-to-day leadership—particularly intimidating.

Facing the idea of handing over your life's work not only confronts you with considerations of your own mortality and the legacy you wish to leave but also stirs up fears of losing control and becoming less relevant to the business. This emotional complexity, combining the fear of loss, grief, and questions about your ongoing role, can make the succession planning process an emotionally charged task that's easy to defer.

For those who have dedicated their heart and soul to building the company, stepping back is not merely a business decision; it's a deeply personal journey through the realities of change and the pursuit of legacy, making it a task that's as emotionally challenging as it is necessary.

4. Lack of a Clear Successor

The belief that one's unique contributions to a business cannot be matched often stems from the owner's deep involvement in its establishment and growth. This conviction, where personal identity and business success are deeply entangled, can obstruct the process of selecting a successor and obscure the need for the business's sustainability without its founder.

Owners who see themselves as irreplaceable may find it hard to delegate and invest in coaching future leaders, hindering the development of a robust leadership structure. This mindset is further solidified by psychological hurdles such as fear of becoming obsolete, losing one's identity, and reluctance to face retirement. These challenges can delay or complicate the vital steps needed to prepare the business for a future beyond the original owner, making succession planning even more difficult.

5. Concern for the Stakeholders

Stakeholder considerations—including customers, employees, and the local community—significantly influence how you approach succession planning. The priority placed on these groups affects both daily operations and strategic decisions about future leadership.

As an owner, you've likely forged deep connections with your customers through years of personal service and trust. The worry that a change in leadership could weaken these relationships or diminish service quality often leads to hesitation in starting succession plans. This hesitation stems from a desire to maintain customer trust and loyalty.

Similarly, loyal employees are more than just staff; they're part of your extended family, especially in closely-knit teams. There's a genuine concern about how changes in leadership might affect their job security, morale, and well-being. The possibility that a successor might not uphold the same employee-centric values or understand the company culture can delay succession planning.

Furthermore, your business likely plays a crucial role in your community, bolstering the local economy, engaging in community events, and sometimes offering vital services. Owners are acutely aware of their business's community impact and may worry that succession could negatively alter their level of contribution or engagement, affecting the community they value.

6. No One Values My Business

On more than one occasion clients have shared with us stories that mirror the following:

After dedicating their life to building and operating a small business, they find themself at a crossroads, driven by weariness and the inevitable passing of time.

When making the difficult decision to sell the business, they are confronted with a harsh reality: there is little interest in what they have spent their lifetime creating. This realization is an emotional rollercoaster as their life's work seems undervalued—their disappointment stemming from the lack of a successor to carry on their legacy, and their frustration directed at the overall situation.

Your journey through entrepreneurship was more than just a career; it was a passion and a calling that defined much of your identity and existence. The thought of the business coming to an end—not with a bang, but a thud—is a source of deep sorrow. This transitional phase, marked by the struggle to find a buyer who sees the value in your life's work, mirrors the larger existential challenge of facing your mortality and the legacy left behind.

The emotional toll is compounded by the realization that everything you have worked for appears to be fading into obscurity. The decision to sell feels like an admission of defeat, a final acknowledgment that the time has come to let go, not on your terms, but out of necessity. This combination of hurt, disappointment, and frustration highlights the harsh truth that nothing lasts forever.

As we conclude this chapter, consider Gandalf's words from J.R.R. Tolkien's *The Lord of the Rings: The Fellowship of the Ring*:

"All we have to decide is what to do with the time that is given us."

As human beings with finite lifespans, we naturally fear the end of our timeline, which we are blind to. But we cannot fight the passage of time. We only have the choice of maximizing the time we have left or grieving the inevitable.

The urgency and responsibility of pivotal decisions, including succession planning, can either be a point of grief, seen as the tragic end of a heroic story, or it can be seen as the turning point before the peaceful epilogue, an epilogue the hero *made* peaceful with their choices of how to spend their remaining time. The need for effective succession planning to ensure business continuity and legacy preservation is a necessity that will not budge, just as the clock continues to tick, unhindered by our feelings toward it. At some point, if we desire a fruitful, satisfying conclusion to the entrepreneur's experience, we must face it in spite of our feelings.

If you're ready to face it, I'll walk you through the process. You are not alone in this. Everyone has to go through succession planning at some point, and I'm here to help you through it. Find out more in the next chapter.

CHAPTER 2

Family Business' Dirty Little Secret

In our quest to uncover the secrets of business longevity, we delved into the narratives of businesses, especially those that have defied the odds, thriving into the fourth generation of ownership.

These rare gems, comprising merely 3% of companies, hold invaluable lessons for future prosperity. Among them is Diamond Resources, a business services company based in Illinois, founded in the early 1900s. This company's journey from its inception by a visionary founder to its current fourth-generation leadership exemplifies the essence of sustainable business practices and family cohesion.

The company's success story is marked by strategic generational transitions, beginning with the founder's foresight to involve his sons in the business, cultivating a culture of strong relationships and intentional leadership development. As generations succeeded, the family business evolved, incorporating formal structures like Business Governance and Family Governance policies, while maintaining a commitment to core values and open communication. This foundation facilitated seamless transitions through economic downturns and shifts in market demand, allowing for continuous innovation and expansion.

The fourth generation now at the helm embodies the legacy of their great-grandfather's vision, steering the company toward technological advancement and market diversification. Their journey underscores several critical takeaways for enduring business success: the importance of visionary leadership, the value of continuous learning, the necessity of establishing structured governance, the power of family unity, the benefits of early generational engagement, and the significance of mentorship and innovation.

The delicate process of transitioning a family-owned business from one generation to the next involves much more than the mere transfer of responsibilities and assets. For the rest of this chapter, we are going to dive into the individual perspectives of both parents and their next generation, where we uncover a complex landscape of emotional and interpersonal issues.

Each element, from the expectation of legacy and succession to the finer points of communication and relationship dynamics, plays a crucial role in shaping the future of your business. Furthermore, the great divide in values and vision for the future highlights the need for a balanced approach that respects the traditions of the past while embracing innovative changes. This exploration will provide you with a comprehensive understanding of the multifaceted challenges and opportunities that lie ahead within generational succession.

We will begin with the main four points where relationship dynamics may diverge.

Expectations of Legacy and Succession

Parents' Perspective:

Today's generation often views the family business as a significant legacy and a testament to years of hard work and dedication. They likely hold the expectation that their successors will take over and continue to expand the business, honoring the family's history. This expectation is deeply rooted in a traditional sense of familial duty and continuity, where passing down the business is seen as both a privilege and a significant responsibility.

This expectation is accompanied by a profound emotional investment. They have spent considerable time building the business, overcoming numerous challenges, and achieving milestones that have not only supported their family, but also contributed to their community's success.

Next Generation's Perspective:

Conversely, the next generation may not view the inheritance of the family business with the same sense of obligation or desire. Growing up in a different era, their aspirations are influenced by global connectivity, diverse opportunities, and a shift toward personal fulfillment that doesn't necessarily align with running a family business. They feel that their ambitions and skills are better suited to different industries or ventures that are more in tune with contemporary markets or their personal interests.

Additionally, many recognize the hard work their parents put into the business and have felt the impact of their parents' absence, witnessing firsthand the physical, emotional, and financial stress that comes with business ownership.

Communication and Relationship Dynamics

Parents' Perspective:

Parents who have built the family business tend to have a traditional approach to communication, often characterized by more hierarchical and less frequent but formal interactions. They believe they are communicating effectively by simply passing down orders or making decisions without extensive consultation. From their perspective, they have the family's best interests at heart, and their experience justifies a more directive style of communication. Parents assume that their decisions will be accepted without question, reflecting a time when traditional business practices didn't require as much collaborative dialogue.

This approach can create challenges when younger family members, who may expect a more inclusive and transparent style of communication, are coming into the business. Parents feel frustrated when they perceive resistance or a lack of enthusiasm from the next generation, misunderstanding it as a lack of commitment or respect rather than a response to the communication style.

Next Generation's Perspective:

The next generation approaches business with modern ideas influenced by current management and communication trends, which emphasize openness, regular feedback, and collaborative decision-making. They prefer ongoing dialogue and more decentralized organization that allow for greater involvement in decision-making processes. This generation finds the traditional, top-down communication approach to be restrictive and uninviting, which can lead to feelings of being undervalued or excluded from truly contributing to the business's future.

When their need for open communication and involvement is not met, it leads to mistrust toward the parents' intentions or doubts about their own place within the company. They suspect their parents are unwilling to adapt or that they are not being prepared adequately for future leadership roles. This perceived lack of transparency and inclusion erodes trust and hinders effective collaboration.

Divergence in Values and Vision for the Future

Parents' Perspective:

The divergence in values and vision between parents and the next generation often presents challenges in family-owned businesses. Parents typically prioritize business continuity, favoring established practices and traditional success metrics like financial growth and market expansion. This conservative approach stems from a belief in the effectiveness of proven methods and a cautious attitude toward risk, aiming to preserve stability and protect the business's legacy.

A parent's skepticism toward radical changes reflects their commitment not just to family, but also to employees and stakeholders, including the broader community. While this ensures a stable foundation, it can clash with the innovative ideas from younger family members, creating potential friction that must be carefully managed to maintain the business's health and longevity.

Next Generation's Perspective:

The next generation of leaders brings a perspective that significantly shifts the focus toward contemporary values and priorities. They champion a more holistic approach to business management, emphasizing not just profit but also the broader impact of their decisions on their family, employees, customers, and the environment. This includes a strong commitment to sustainability, aiming to incorporate environmentally friendly practices across all levels of the business.

The next generation is seen steering family businesses towards a future where financial success is balanced with positive impacts on society and the environment. By embracing sustainability, work-life harmony, social responsibility, and technological advancements, they are redefining what it means to run a successful family business in the modern world.

Recognition of Sacrifice and Contribution

Parents' Perspective:

Many parents involved in family-owned businesses view their long-term commitment and hard work as not just professional responsibilities, but as significant personal sacrifices made for the benefit of their family, especially their children. This sense of sacrifice reflects countless hours of dedication that go beyond the usual demands of running a business. Parents often perceive this effort as laying a robust foundation for their children's future, ensuring that the next generation inherits a stable, thriving enterprise.

Consequently, they expect a degree of gratitude and acknowledgment from their children, hoping for recognition of their labor and sacrifices. This expectation creates a strong emotional underpinning to the generational handover, with parents viewing their dedication as a pivotal element of their children's eventual success and well-being.

Next Generation's Perspective:

The next generation sees these sacrifices differently. They often witness the personal costs, including physical and financial stress, health issues, and strained family relationships, that these sacrifices entail. Rather than viewing the business as a gift, they see it as a burden that could potentially replicate the same challenges in their lives. This perspective makes them wary of stepping into roles that seem to demand the same level of personal sacrifice.

In addition to the main factors already discussed, several other elements are crucial to understanding the complexity of generational transitions in family-owned businesses. Addressing these additional factors can provide a more comprehensive view of the potential gaps and challenges.

Role Competence and Preparation

Parents' Perspective:

In family-owned businesses, parents often expect the next generation will naturally acquire the necessary skills and knowledge to run the company simply by being around the business operation. This expectation can lead parents to underestimate the importance of education, formal training, and practical experience in different roles within the company.

This approach can lead to significant gaps in the next gen's readiness and expertise, as they lack critical operational, financial, and strategic management skills that are essential for the business's success.

Next Generation's Perspective:

The next generation will experience feelings of unpreparedness or inadequacy in regards to taking over the family business if they have not been systematically involved in its operations or provided with opportunities to learn in a structured and deliberate manner. This lack of preparation leads to doubts about their own competence and readiness for leadership roles within the company.

Additionally, if these young successors have pursued other professional interests or have diverse educational backgrounds that do not align directly with the family business, they feel that their unique skills and experiences are not fully appreciated or utilized. Feeling undervalued makes them hesitant to take on a role that does not seem to match their skills and goals. They will often worry about meeting your expectations, whether stated or implied, and fear the impact of failure personally and professionally.

Cultural and Tech Transformation

Parents' Perspective:

Parents who have successfully managed family businesses over the years show resistance to implementing changes, particularly when it involves adopting new technologies or integrating modern business practices. This hesitance often stems from a deep trust in the "tried and true" methods that have historically sustained the business. For many, these established practices represent more than just operational decisions; they are a legacy of proven success that has built the business's reputation and stability.

Next Generation's Perspective:

The younger generation in family businesses, well-versed in technological advancements and cultural shifts, often identifies opportunities for innovation that their parents might miss. Their familiarity with new trends equips them to propose transformative changes aimed at optimizing operations, expanding market reach, and improving customer engagement.

However, their push for innovation extends beyond technology to include aligning the business with modern ethical standards, sustainability, and global market trends. Resistance to these progressive ideas from the older generation can intensify generational tensions, complicating efforts to maintain a cooperative and harmonious work environment.

Financial Expectations and Realities

Parents' Perspective:

Owners often regard the business as financially stable, having built it to withstand various economic climates while providing a steady source of income. They expect the next generation to not only maintain this stability but to improve upon it, viewing the business as a significant part of the family's wealth and a cornerstone of their retirement planning. According to a survey by Family Business Alliance, about 63% of family business owners depend on their businesses for retirement, reinforcing the expectation of financial security and continuity.

Next Generation's Perspective:

The next generation views the financial landscape through a different lens, especially given the volatile nature of modern markets and rapid technological advancements. They are often concerned about the significant investments needed to modernize the business and keep it competitive, which can be substantial and risky. They are also acutely aware of the broader economic pressures and industry-specific challenges that may not have been as pronounced in the past. As an example, sectors like retail and manufacturing have seen intense disruption from both new technology such as AI and changing consumer behaviors.

A study by McKinsey noted that younger business leaders are more likely to emphasize the importance of investing in new technologies and capabilities to stay relevant, which can be a source of financial strain. They are concerned about the sustainability of the business in a market that is rapidly evolving, questioning whether the business can continue to thrive without significant changes that may require a large financial outlay.

Personal Autonomy and Independence

Parents' Perspective:

Parents who have established and successfully managed a family business tend to prioritize continuity, risk management, and preservation of the established business culture and practices. In their opinion, personal autonomy and independence within the business context are often viewed with caution. They worry that too much independence could lead to decisions that deviate from proven strategies or undermine the business's long-term goals. They prefer a more controlled approach to leadership transitions, where the next gen gradually assimilates into the existing business framework before making any significant changes.

For many parents, the idea of autonomy is linked to responsibilities rather than freedoms. They expect the next generation to earn their autonomy through demonstrated competence and loyalty to the family's ways of doing business. This perspective is grounded in a desire to protect the business's legacy and ensure that it remains stable and profitable for future generations.

Next Generation's Perspective:

The next generation often enters the family business with fresh ideas and a desire to make their mark. Having grown up in a more interconnected and rapidly changing world, they see autonomy and independence as crucial to driving innovation and adapting the business to new market realities. They are likely to value the freedom to explore new opportunities, whether through technological advancements, new market strategies, or alternative business models.

The next gen's concerns regarding autonomy often center around feeling restricted or micromanaged by their parents. They feel that their potential to bring positive change is stifled if they are not given the room to implement their ideas and strategies. This can lead to frustration and a sense of being undervalued, particularly if they have acquired relevant skills and experiences outside the family business that they believe would benefit the enterprise.

Inter-Generational Trust and Respect

Parents' Perspective:

For parents, trust and respect are grounded in their experiences and the proven strategies that helped them grow the business. When considering transitioning their business to the next generation, parents often look for signs that their children respect the legacy and the hard work that has gone into building the business. They value acknowledgment of past successes and the wisdom accumulated over years of growing and managing the company. Parents also equate trust with adherence to established ways of doing business and show hesitation or concern if the next generation pushes for rapid changes or a shift in business direction.

From the parents' perspective, respect is demonstrated through a willingness to learn and take gradual responsibility under their guidance. They expect the next generation to understand and appreciate the complexities of the business before attempting to make their mark. Trust, in this context, involves believing that the next generation will preserve the core values and mission of the business, managing it with the same level of dedication and integrity that they did.

Next Generation's Perspective:

The next generation often seeks recognition for their own capabilities and the fresh perspectives they bring to the table. They feel that respect from their parents should not just be based on their willingness to conform to traditional methods but also on the acknowledgment of their innovative ideas and the unique skills they possess. The next generation sees trust as the freedom to make decisions and implement changes that they believe are necessary for the business's future success, especially in adapting to modern market conditions and technological advancements.

For the next generation, intergenerational respect also includes a degree of autonomy and the opportunity to prove themselves as capable leaders. They desire a collaborative relationship where their views and contributions are taken seriously and where they are trusted to take the business forward without constant oversight or being second-guessed.

What's Next?

In this chapter, we've explored the differing perspectives of parents and the next generation on key issues that often lead to conflict within family-owned businesses, potentially threatening the legacy and succession process. Understanding these differences is essential for balancing the preservation of tradition with the need for innovation.

Moving into Chapter 3, we will introduce practical strategies, tools, and resources that will facilitate a smoother transition and help keep your business within the family. This upcoming chapter will offer actionable advice to align both generations, foster mutual respect and trust, and ensure the continued success of your family business.

CHAPTER 3

How to Keep Your Business "In the Family"

In Chapter 2, we highlighted the journey of a successful transition by Diamond Resources from the first to the fourth generation in a family-owned business, highlighting key takeaways and common conflict points. As we delve deeper into Chapter 3, our focus shifts to strategies and essential resources designed to enhance the likelihood of a successful family business transition.

Maintaining healthy family relationships is as vital as ensuring the business's ongoing success during these transitions. Family conflicts often arise from differing opinions, visions, values, or unresolved issues, which can heighten emotions, cloud judgment, and divert focus from the goal of a successful transition. This book aims to provide guidance on bridging these gaps personally and professionally. Our structured approach not only aids in crafting a resilient succession plan but also fosters unity, ensuring that the business thrives *and* relationships are preserved for future generations.

Continuing a business within the family often necessitates uncomfortable but crucial actions. Are you ready?

Consider the case of Bennett Farms, a sprawling family enterprise deeply rooted in golden wheat fields. For Charles and Julie Bennett, the farm was more than a business; it was their home and legacy, earmarked for generational succession. Despite their aspirations, the realization that their sons might choose different paths struck Charles with profound sorrow.

Initially, Charles avoided succession discussions, hoping his sons' life paths would naturally lead back to the farm. However, the turning point came when we facilitated crucial conversations between Charles, Julie, and their sons, Tim and Matt, who had pursued careers in business and marketing, respectively.

The initial meeting was charged with tension and unspoken expectations. As mediators, Julie and I carefully navigated these dynamics, focusing on eliciting deep questions, practicing active listening, and fostering empathy. Occasional breaks were implemented to maintain productivity.

To deepen our understanding and mitigate emotional volatility, we introduced a behavioral assessment tool toward the end of the session. Scheduled for use in their second meeting, this tool aims to foster open discussions and provide insights into each family member's decision-making process, conflict resolution style, communication habits, and personal preferences. It also gave clarity as to why Tim and Matt were drawn to careers outside of their family farm operation.

Through a series of strategic meetings, the Bennett family embarked on a transformative journey to reimagine their family farm. With the team's guidance, they explored potential partnerships and business models that could integrate Tim and Matt's external passions with the farm's operations. This process involved innovative approaches to keep the farm within the family while adapting to today's demands and opportunities.

This transition required a thoughtful restructuring of roles and responsibilities. Charles continued to oversee traditional operations but with a reduced workload to accommodate his age. Tim, with a keen interest in technology, led the integration of advanced agricultural tech to optimize crop yields and reduce expenses. Matt, motivated by sustainable practices, proposed eco-friendly techniques and explored transitioning to organic certification for a part of the farm.

As we guided the Bennetts through this intricate transition, the key to success became evident: their ability to embrace change while respecting their roots. Each meeting built on the previous one, gradually forming a comprehensive strategy that promised to keep the farm relevant and thriving in a changing agricultural landscape.

Top 10 Issues to Address During Succession Conversations

When having intergenerational family conversations about succession planning in a family-owned business, several key issues commonly arise. Preparing for these can help ensure smoother transitions and better outcomes.

Here are 10 issues you should be prepared to address.

1. **Vision for the Future**

   Each generation has varying visions for the future of the business. It's important to discuss these openly to understand everyone's expectations and aspirations, with the desired result aligning everyone on the vision of the company.

2. **Roles and Responsibilities**

   Clarity of roles and responsibilities after the transition is crucial. This includes defining new roles for outgoing members if they plan to stay involved, based on the business needs and their unique talents.

3. **Leadership Style**

   Discuss how leadership styles will change with new management. The incoming generation will have different approaches to leadership and management that need to be acknowledged and integrated.

4. **Financial Expectations**

   Expectations regarding profit distribution, reinvestment, and personal financial planning are often contentious. Transparent discussions about finances can prevent misunderstandings.

5. Conflict Resolution

Establish a process for resolving disputes. Introducing neutral third-party mediators should be a strategy to consider.

6. Training and Development

Address the need for training and preparation for those taking on new roles, including the possibility of external education or internal mentoring.

7. Cultural and Value Differences

Generational shifts bring changes in company culture and values. These shifts need to be called out and managed carefully to maintain identity while still evolving.

8. Retirement and Exit Strategies

For outgoing family members, discussing retirement plans and exit strategies is essential. This includes financial security and the emotional aspects of leaving the business.

9. Legal and Estate Planning

Ensure all legalities are addressed, including wills, trusts, and ownership documents. Legal clarity will prevent many potential conflicts.

10. Recognition and Legacy

Discuss how the contributions of outgoing family members will be recognized. This will respect their legacy and reinforce their value to the business and family.

Addressing these issues in a structured and respectful manner can help ensure that the business transition strengthens rather than strains your family's ties. Ensuring that each family member feels heard and valued during succession planning discussions is crucial for maintaining harmony and achieving a successful transition.

Assessment Tools for Effective Family Business Transitions

Earlier in this chapter, we discussed using an assessment tool with the Bennett family and its purpose. We highly recommend employing such a tool as you develop your succession plan. These tools are invaluable, offering deep insights and fostering open communication. They help eliminate emotional triggers and enhance respect among family members.

Based on our experience, these are assessments we recommend:

1. **Predictive Index**

   Useful for determining role alignment, conflict resolution, enhanced communication, and leadership development within family businesses. https://www. predictiveindex.com/

2. **Hogan Motives, Values, Preferences Inventory (MVPI)**

   Sheds light on underlying values and preferences, aiding in aligning the business with individual motivations. https://www.hoganassessments.com/

3. **CliftonStrengths**

   Identifies an individual's top strengths and talents, helping to assign roles within the business that capitalize on each family member's capabilities. https://www. gallup.com/cliftonstrengths/en/252137/home.aspx

4. **DISC Assessment**

   Categorizes individuals into four primary behavioral styles, providing insights into communication patterns and preferred working styles. https://www.discprofile. com/what-is-disc

5. **Myers-Briggs Type Indicator (MBTI)**

Reveals individual preferences in decision-making, energy sources, and problem-solving approaches. https://www.myersbriggs.org/my-mbti-personality-type/myers-briggs-overview/

6. **Six Seconds Emotional Intelligence Assessment**

Provides insights into how individuals manage their emotions and interact with others, useful in creating harmonious communication within family businesses. https://www.6seconds.org/

7. **Thrive / Wither Zones**

The Thrive/Wither Zones exercise, featured in Gary Frey's book "Silence the Imposter: 7 Weapons To Silence Imposter Syndrome," addresses a common challenge potential successors may encounter: imposter syndrome upon assuming the new role. amzn.to/3Y46kLD

Another effective tool for you and your family to use as you work through the conversations and evaluation process is called The Johari Window. This concept was shared with me by Nick Whitney, Professional EOS Implementer in Charlotte, NC, and it has proved to be very helpful for both individuals and leadership teams.

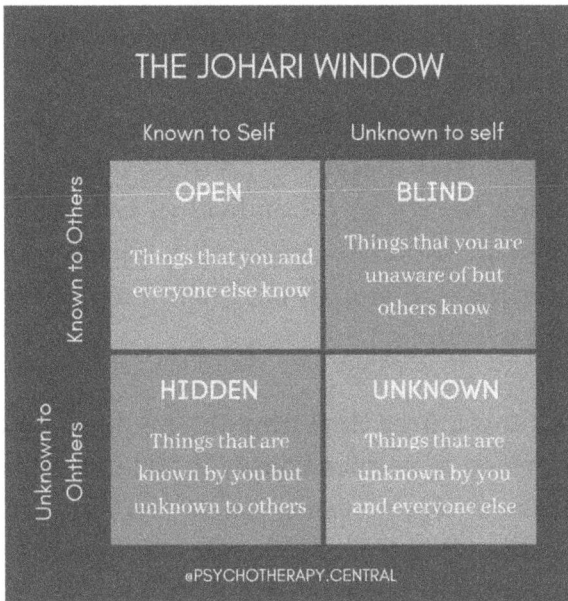

THE JOHARI WINDOW

	Known to Self	Unknown to self
Known to Others	**OPEN** — Things that you and everyone else know	**BLIND** — Things that you are unaware of but others know
Unknown to Ohthers	**HIDDEN** — Things that are known by you but unknown to others	**UNKNOWN** — Things that are unknown by you and everyone else

@PSYCHOTHERAPY.CENTRAL

The Johari Window is a psychological model developed by Joseph Luft and Harrington Ingham in 1955. It's designed to help individuals understand their relationships with themselves and others. The model consists of four quadrants, representing different aspects of information about oneself:

1. **Open Area (Arena):** This quadrant contains information known to both the individual and others, representing aspects of personality, behavior, attitudes, feelings, and motivations that are openly shared and understood.

2. **Blind Area (Blind Spot):** This quadrant contains information known to others but not to the individual themselves. These are aspects of one's personality or

behavior that others perceive but of which the individual may be unaware.

3. **Hidden Area (Facade):** This quadrant contains information known to the individual but not to others. These are aspects of personality, feelings, or experiences that individuals choose to keep private or disclose selectively.

4. **Unknown Area (Unknown):** This quadrant contains information neither known to the individual nor to others. It represents aspects of the individual's personality, potential, or behavior that have not yet been discovered or recognized.

The Johari Window is often used in self-awareness exercises, team building, and interpersonal communication workshops to enhance understanding, empathy, and collaboration among individuals or groups. Through feedback and self-disclosure, the goal is to expand the open area, reduce blind spots, and increase mutual understanding and trust.

This is how Emily, Founder of Sweet Treats Bakery, used the Johari Window.

Johari Window Case Study

As the sun set on another busy day at her family-owned bakery, Emily sat down at her desk with a stack of papers in front of her. She felt the weight of responsibility as the sole owner of

Sweet Treats Bakery. At 60 years old, she knew it was time to start thinking about the future of her business.

With her mind set on developing a succession plan, she recalled a workshop she attended years ago on communication and self-awareness, and she retrieved her notes regarding the Johari Window exercise.

Emily began by examining the "Open Area" of the Johari Window—the aspects of her business that were known to both her and her employees. Here, she listed the strengths and weaknesses of each member of her staff, considering their skills, experience, and potential for leadership roles. She realized that some of her employees possessed talents she hadn't fully recognized, opening up new possibilities for succession.

Moving to the "Blind Area," Emily considered the perspectives of her employees. She asked for feedback on their perceptions of the business and its future leadership. Surprisingly, she discovered that some employees saw potential in individuals she hadn't considered for leadership roles. This expanded her pool of potential successors and challenged her assumptions about who might be the best fit.

In the "Hidden Area," Emily confronted her own fears and insecurities about stepping back from the business. She acknowledged her reluctance to let go of control and her concerns about finding someone capable of upholding the bakery's legacy. This reflection allowed her to address her reservations and communicate more openly with her family and employees about her succession plans.

Finally, in the "Unknown Area," Emily considered the untapped potential within her business. She realized that by fostering a culture of mentorship and professional development, she could uncover hidden talents and groom future leaders from within her team. This realization inspired her to create training programs and opportunities for her employees to grow and take on greater responsibilities.

Armed with insights from the Johari Window exercise, Emily crafted a comprehensive succession plan that honored the bakery's legacy while embracing the potential for growth and change. By leveraging the power of self-awareness and open communication, she ensured a smooth transition and a bright future for Sweet Treats Bakery.

Moving Forward, Keep In Mind...

Keeping a business within the family involves balancing the technical aspects of succession planning with the emotional and relational dynamics of the family. By utilizing third-party facilitators, recognizing generational differences, using objective assessment tools, and prioritizing family relationships, you can set the stage for a successful transition that honors both the family's legacy and its future.

As we proceed, it is essential to remain committed to maintaining family dynamics and relationships, especially when determining whether the next generation is the right candidate to become the successor. This chapter aims to equip you with the tools and understanding needed to navigate these waters, ensuring that your family business not only survives, but thrives, through transitional phases.

Up next, we'll talk about seven successful methods of transition that will eliminate some of the stress of searching for succession candidates.

CHAPTER 4

Finding Your MVB
(Most Valuable Buyer)

In the face of sobering statistics revealing that 70% of small family-owned businesses[4] in the United States falter as they transition from the first generation to the next, it's crucial to consider a variety of exit strategies.

The importance of small businesses in job creation and their role in sustaining the economy cannot be overstated; their growth is crucial for the nation's employment health and overall economic prosperity. To prevent failure post-transition, a proper succession plan must account for possible business transitions outside of the generational handoff.

This chapter explores seven popular strategies for business owners facing the challenging decision of how to successfully exit or transform their family-owned business. While the romantic notion of passing the business from one generation

---

[4] SBA

to the next remains appealing, modern circumstances and market dynamics often dictate a different approach.

Current Partners

Jeni meticulously planned her succession to ensure her business thrived beyond her leadership. She chose to transition ownership to her partners, who were deeply familiar with the firm's culture and operations. This approach facilitated a smooth transition, supported by a buy-sell agreement, which kept costs low and maintained client and employee confidence.

However, the process was not without challenges. The sale price was lower than potential external offers, influenced by the partners' knowledge of the business's weaknesses. Additionally, the transition revealed hidden conflicts and competency gaps among the partners, straining relationships and exposing deficiencies in handling key business areas. The proceeds from the sale were realized more slowly than expected, dependent on the business's performance and the partners' financial capacity to complete the buyout.

This example underscores that while transferring ownership within a small business can minimize disruption, it demands strategic planning and clear communication to address the inherent complexities and ensure the business's sustained success. Additionally, constructing a buy-sell agreement with an established valuation process well in advance will benefit the seller.

Key Leader within the Company

Ashley, who founded a successful graphic design firm, decided to retire after two decades and chose to transition ownership to Mark, her creative director and a key employee of over ten years. This decision leveraged Mark's deep understanding of the business and maintained continuity, as he was already well-integrated with the firm's operations and culture. The transition allowed Ashley to gradually mentor Mark into his new role, ensuring a smooth handover.

However, the transition posed challenges. Mark struggled to balance his existing duties with his new responsibilities as a future owner, impacting his focus. Financially, Mark couldn't afford a substantial upfront purchase, necessitating significant seller financing from Ashley, which introduced financial risks dependent on the continued success of the business under Mark's leadership. Additionally, Mark faced a steep learning curve in areas like finance and strategic planning, revealing gaps in his experience.

This scenario highlights the importance of balancing the benefits of operational continuity and employee motivation against the risks of financial instability and management inexperience in succession planning. For business owners like Ashley, it's essential to adopt a well-thought-out strategy and maintain transparent communication to safeguard both the business's continuity and her financial well-being.

Leadership Team

As I sat down with George, a seasoned business owner ready to transition his family-owned business to his leadership team, he shared his thoughtful approach and the strategic concerns surrounding the decision. The setting was intimate, reflective of the deep personal connections he had cultivated within his business. George began by expressing a strong sense of trust in his leadership team, who had been integral to the day-to-day operations and were deeply familiar with the company's core values and vision.

He emphasized the benefits of this succession strategy, noting the continuity it promised and how it naturally boosted employee morale. "By transferring ownership internally, I am not just passing on a business, but a legacy," George explained. "It ensures that the business remains in hands that value and understand its heritage, and this continuity is vital for both our clients and our team."

However, George was candid about the challenges as well. He pointed out that shared ownership could lead to complicated decision-making dynamics and potential conflicts if not managed correctly. "It's crucial to establish a clear governance structure," he advised. "Setting up a board or implementing a systematic review process helps in maintaining direction and unity." He also highlighted the importance of infusing new ideas into the business to avoid becoming insular, suggesting that bringing in external advisors or board members could provide fresh perspectives and drive innovation.

Financial stability was another critical aspect of the transition. George planned to structure the sale as an internal buyout, which would provide him with a stable, gradual income while safeguarding the business's financial health. This method, he noted, aligned the sale with the business's cash flow, easing the financial burden on the new owners and ensuring a smoother transition.

Throughout our discussion, George's insights painted a picture of a carefully considered succession plan that balanced the emotional and financial aspects of passing on a family business. His experience offered valuable lessons on the complexities of such a transition, emphasizing the importance of preparation, clear communication, and flexibility in succession planning.

Employee Stock Ownership Plan (ESOP)

When Robert, the founder of a mid-sized tech company, decided to retire, he chose to transition ownership through an Employee Stock Ownership Plan (ESOP). This plan allowed employees to buy shares with pre-tax dollars, offered Robert tax deferrals on gains, and motivated employees to think like owners, fostering a sense of continuity and commitment.

However, setting up and maintaining the ESOP proved costly and complex, requiring ongoing management, and obligating the company to buy back shares from departing employees. Despite these challenges, the ESOP helped preserve the company's family-like culture and ensured a gradual, stable transition as Robert stepped away. This approach reflects a thoughtful balance between empowering employees and managing the financial and administrative complexities inherent in ESOPs.

To learn more details about an ESOP, visit:
https://bit.ly/3VSxO5M.

Private Equity

While sitting across from David, a seasoned business owner who had recently transitioned his family-owned business to a Private Equity firm, everyone in the room could see the stress that remained on David's face. He was there to share his experience and the wisdom he learned as he completed the sale of his company.

David outlined the positives of engaging with the Private Equity firm with a clear tone of practicality and hindsight. "The partnership with the firm brought substantial capital infusion and professional management into our business," he stated. "This not only accelerated our growth trajectory but also expanded our market presence significantly. The expertise they brought in leveled up our operations, introducing advanced performance metrics and operational efficiencies that were beyond our previous capabilities."

However, David also delved into the challenges. "There were considerable trade-offs," he admitted. "The firm's drive to maximize returns often clashed with our family-oriented values. This approach led to decisions that were tough on a personal level, including layoffs and shifts in company culture that prioritized profitability over employee relations."

He continued, emphasizing the loss of control. "Surrendering operational and strategic control was challenging. The firm set aggressive financial targets, and the pressure to meet these was a stark contrast to how we previously managed our business. It's a different kind of pressure than what a family business is used to handling."

In summary, selling to a PE firm can yield significant financial and professional growth but involves major shifts that can affect your legacy and the company's future. The process of closing a deal with a PE firm can be lengthy and is generally the most expensive option, yet it often results in a higher sale price, providing substantial financial benefits. However, these deals can also be very difficult to finalize. Thorough due diligence and a clear understanding of the PE firm's strategy are essential to effectively balance these factors and navigate the complexities of the transaction.

Merge with Another Company or Strategic Partner

In the fast-paced world of software development, CT was the visionary founder of a niche software company which specialized in educational software tools. With his retirement looming on the horizon, CT began contemplating the future trajectory of his business. Aware of the increasing competitive pressures and the need for more robust resources to innovate and expand, CT viewed a merger not just as an exit strategy, but as a vital step for the survival and growth of his company.

When you decide to merge your business with another company or strategic partner, you significantly alter the ownership structure and business trajectory. This move can drive transformative growth by opening new avenues, expanding into new markets, enhancing competitiveness, and accessing new customer bases. The influx of resources from a larger or strategically aligned partner can also accelerate innovation and product development, increasing the business's value and providing substantial financial benefits, either as a lucrative exit strategy or an opportunity for reinvestment.

However, merging involves extensive and costly due diligence, including legal, financial, and operational assessments. It also poses potential challenges, such as disrupting employee morale, customer relationships, and operational continuity. Additionally, there's a risk of not achieving anticipated synergies, which can devalue the original business' contributions and potentially jeopardize the future of the merged entity.

The emotional impact of losing independence and merging into a different corporate culture should not be underestimated. Nonetheless, merging offers the potential to see your business evolve into a more impactful entity, allowing you to maintain involvement and contribute your expertise.

In summary, while a merger offers a pathway to significant growth and a potentially rewarding financial exit, it comes with risks that need meticulous management. The process requires a strategic vision that aligns with both your goals and the business's long-term viability, acknowledging that despite the potential benefits, studies such as those from the Harvard

Business Review indicate that 70-90% of mergers fail to meet expectations. This reality underscores the importance of careful planning and execution to ensure successful integration and realization of merger goals.

Hybrid Ownership Structures

In the evolving landscape of small business ownership and succession planning, the hybrid model has become an increasingly popular strategy. This approach combines two distinct transition methods, such as merging with another company while incorporating an Employee Stock Ownership Plan (ESOP) or involving both family members and private equity investors. This tailored method allows owners to balance personal, financial, and operational goals with the future viability of their business.

The following story is an example of how the hybrid succession plan worked for our clients in Kentucky.

Hops & Barley, founded by college friends Alex and Jamie, was at a crossroads as the founders neared retirement. Their objectives included preserving their legacy and expanding their reach by merging with a larger regional brewery that supported local brewers and provided necessary capital. Simultaneously, they established an Employee Stock Ownership Plan (ESOP) to involve their dedicated employees in the company's future success.

This transition brought significant benefits. The merger provided the capital needed for growth and allowed Alex and

Jamie to gradually reduce their day-to-day involvement while maintaining the brewery's brand continuity. The ESOP created a sense of ownership among employees, fostering loyalty and motivation.

However, the transition also posed challenges. Merging different company cultures and systems risked operational difficulties, and the larger company's strategic goals could have potentially overshadowed Hops & Barley's mission. Additionally, managing an ESOP required ongoing legal and financial oversight, adding complexity and expense.

Despite these concerns, the merger allowed Hops & Barley to maintain its unique identity and creative freedom. Alex and Jamie allocated a substantial portion of their new company shares to the ESOP, giving employees from brewmasters to sales teams a stake in the company. This not only motivated the team but also gave them a say in the brewery's future.

Ultimately, the success of the merger and ESOP was clear. Hops & Barley kept its original charm and continued to innovate, with employees benefiting significantly from their stake in the company. Alex and Jamie's strategy ensured the brewery's sustained success for future generations.

To Summarize…

As we close Chapter 4 on finding your Most Valuable Buyer, recall how we have navigated through the complex terrain of exiting or transforming family-owned businesses. Each approach has its own set of benefits—such as ensuring continuity, maintaining company culture, or unlocking new growth opportunities—while also presenting unique challenges that require attention to detail and careful strategic planning. By understanding the nuances of each option, you can make an informed decision that secures your financial future and your life's work.

Below is a summary of each buyer method with its unique challenges and advantages.

Buyer Options	Options	What is it	When should I consider	Advantages	Considerations
Family Succession	Transfer to Family Member(s)	Passing the business on to a family member or members	When there is a capable and willing family member; Desire to keep the business in the family	Continuity of family legacy; Retains family control and culture	Potential family conflicts; Need for clear succession planning and training
Management Buyout (MBO)	Sale to Existing Management Team	Selling the business to the current management team	When you want to ensure continuity and reward your management team	Smooth transition; Continuity in business operations	Financing might be challenging; Management team's ability to run the business independently
Employee Stock Ownership Plan (ESOP)	Sale to Employees via ESOP	Selling the business to employees through a trust that buys shares on their behalf	When aiming to reward employees and ensure business continuity	Increased employee motivation and retention; Potential tax benefits	Complex and costly to set up; Requires ongoing administration and compliance
Financial Buyer	Private Equity or Investment Groups	Selling your business to investment firms that aim to grow and later resell the business	When seeking capital for growth or partial liquidity while retaining some control	Access to capital for growth; Potential for significant expertise in scaling businesses	Focus on ROI which might lead to aggressive cost-cutting; Shorter investment horizon
Strategic Buyer	Sale to a Competitor or Complementary Business	Selling your business to a company in the same industry or a related field	When looking for a buyer who understands the industry and can integrate your business easily	High likelihood of understanding and valuing synergies; Potentially higher purchase price	Potential for cultural clashes; Risk of layoffs or restructuring

As we delve into Chapter 5, we turn our focus to the pivotal process of developing a successful succession plan. Here, we will explore the various approaches you might take when deciding to start this journey, each with its distinct advantages and challenges.

CHAPTER 5

How to Make It Happen

Succession planning is a critical component of any business's longevity and stability, but approaches can vary widely based on the business's needs and the owner's preferences. This chapter explores four distinct strategies for succession planning, each with its own set of challenges and benefits.

First, we consider the "Ostrich Strategy," where business owners, like John Carter of BuildRight Construction, delay planning due to time constraints, leaving their operations vulnerable to unforeseen disruptions. Second, we discuss the "DIY Succession Planning" approach as exemplified by Tom, who inherited his father's law firm and initially struggled without professional guidance.

Third, we explore the benefits of developing an "Internal Dream Team" to handle succession planning, a method chosen by Jordan, owner of a thriving Employee Benefits firm. Finally, we look at the advantages of hiring a "Third-Party Consultant or Coach," a strategy employed by Sam, an electrical contractor in South Carolina, to ensure unbiased and effective planning.

Each of these strategies offers insights into the complexities of preparing for business continuity and the transfer of leadership.

The Four Main Succession Planning Approaches and Their Consequences

Ostrich Strategy (Sticking Your Head in the Sand)

Have you ever found yourself putting off important decisions until "there's more time," or maybe you just aren't ready to deal with it yet?

You're not alone. Many fall prey to what's often dubbed the "Ostrich Strategy"—burying one's head in the sand to avoid current issues.

Take John Carter of BuildRight Construction, for example. Convinced he'd tackle succession planning when less busy, John always told himself, "I'll get to it as soon as I free up some time." Unfortunately, this method exposes the business to a wide range of risks.

When he lost a key employee due to unclear future roles within the company, the realization hit him hard. Overwhelmed with deep regret, anger at himself for not addressing the issue sooner, and frustration over the avoidable disruption, John saw firsthand how his delay impacted his operations and exposed vulnerabilities in his management approach.

This loss underscored the critical importance of transparent communication and proactive planning. Without a clear succession plan, any sudden mishap could disrupt operations, erode employee morale, and give competitors a chance to snatch human capital or market share.

Could this be the approach you're unintentionally taking? Our 2023 study revealed that a significant number of business owners default to this strategy, either by choice or circumstance. It's crucial to recognize that waiting for the "right time" might lead to missing out on securing your business's future. Let's explore why proactive planning is the safer route and how you can avoid falling into the ostrich trap.

DIY Succession Planning

Why do business owners often choose the DIY approach to succession planning? Many believe it saves money and that they can manage the complexities themselves with the help of their leadership teams.

But what are the real consequences of this choice?

Consider the case of Tom, who inherited his father's law firm and was determined to handle the succession planning on his own. Despite his best intentions, Tom quickly discovered the task's complexity. Lacking professional guidance, he encountered numerous missteps, causing frequent delays as he tried to rectify his mistakes.

After a grueling eighteen months, Tom finally hired a specialist in succession planning. This expert introduced a well-defined process and tailored strategies that revitalized Tom's efforts. Reflecting on his experience, Tom realized that seeking professional help from the start would have saved him significant time and money. The modest initial savings from his DIY approach paled in comparison to the benefits of expert advice in preserving his father's legacy.

If you're considering the DIY route, remember that a certain degree of preparation and self-education—such as gathering information, attending webinars, reading books, and consulting with experts—can be beneficial. This approach allows you to become knowledgeable about the process, which is crucial since you'll likely navigate succession planning only once in your lifetime.

However, don't let this initial learning phase turn into procrastination. Recognizing when it's time to seek professional assistance can make the difference between preserving a legacy and jeopardizing your business's future.

Develop an Internal Dream Team

Have you ever considered assembling your own "Dream Team" to lead your business's succession planning? Let's take inspiration from Jordan, the owner of a thriving Employee Benefits firm, who recognized the critical need to secure his company's future.

Jordan strategically formed an internal team composed of key senior managers and trusted advisors. This team included Alex, the COO, known for his sharp operational insights; Priya, the HR Director, with a deep understanding of the company culture and its people; and Chris, the Director of Finance, whose expertise in financial stability and risk management proved invaluable. Together, they brought a rich blend of knowledge about the company's operations and history, which is essential for effective planning.

The success of Jordan's team hinged on their ability to critically evaluate and, when necessary, challenge his initial ideas. Their openness ensured that the plan was not only realistic but also comprehensive, addressing all potential challenges and opportunities. By fostering a culture of trust and promoting long-term relationships within the team, they developed a committed and insightful planning process. This approach allowed the team to fully own the plan, positioning them to successfully manage the company's transition when the time came.

Imagine this was your approach. What can you learn from Jordan's strategy to build your own succession planning team? Consider how you can foster a similar environment of trust and critical evaluation among your key players to ensure a seamless transition for your business.

Hiring a Third-Party Consultant or Coach

In the Lowcountry of South Carolina, Sam, a seasoned electrical contractor, faced the sensitive and complex task of planning for the future of his business. Recognizing the complexities and emotional weight of discussing succession with his family and team, Sam made a strategic decision. He brought in a neutral third-party consultant, an expert in family business transitions, to guide the discussions. This wasn't just any consultant, but a seasoned mediator who specialized in family business transitions. This consultant provided an unbiased perspective, skillfully navigated tough conversations, and shed light on issues that had previously gone unnoticed.

As the meetings unfolded, the consultant's expertise kept the discussions focused and productive. These initial talks transformed into decisive actions that effectively safeguarded the future of Sam's business without disrupting his daily responsibilities. This careful orchestration ensured that the succession plan was not only initiated but also brought to successful fruition, securing the legacy of Sam's life's work.

What Results Should You Be Looking For?

Embarking on a succession plan is a once-in-a-lifetime endeavor for most business owners, and getting it right the first time is crucial. While the allure of cost savings through DIY methods or internal efforts can be tempting, the stakes are simply too high. Investing in a professional to help navigate this complex process not only secures your business's legacy but also offers peace of mind that every detail is carefully considered and executed.

What should be the result of such an investment? A comprehensive, legally sound, and financially smart succession plan that aligns with your long-term goals for your family and stakeholders. How might bringing in external expertise transform your approach to securing your business's future?

As we delve into the realm of succession planning, it becomes evident that each strategy, from the risky "Ostrich Strategy" to the careful selection of a third-party consultant, offers its own set of advantages and challenges. The choice of how to handle succession planning is critical and should reflect a thoughtful, proactive approach.

You might choose to manage the process internally, start it on your own, or seek external guidance right from the start. Each method has its merits, but the crucial factor is recognizing the importance of strategic planning. This decision not only ensures the continuity of your business but also preserves a legacy that truly reflects your vision and values.

As you consider the future of your business, think about how each succession planning approach could cater to your specific needs. The right strategy will not only facilitate a smooth transition but also strengthen your business for future generations. Moving forward, evaluate how each option might serve to achieve a successful and enduring transfer of leadership.

Fifteen Prompts for Personalizing Your Succession Plan

Succession planning is a deeply personal and emotional process that shapes the future trajectory of any family-owned business. As business owners embark on this crucial journey, they face a series of important decisions that will determine the continued prosperity of their business and its transition to future generations.

Critical aspects such as selecting the right successors, assessing their readiness to lead, navigating family dynamics, and addressing legal considerations require meticulous thought and strategic planning. To aid in this process, consider the following key questions that are essential to crafting your personalized succession plan:

1. Who will be the successor(s) and what criteria should be used to select them?
2. Is the selected successor(s) interested and prepared to take on leadership responsibilities?
3. How will the transition impact family relationships?
4. What is the timeline for the succession plan?
5. What is the long-term vision for the family-based firm and how will the succession plan align with it?
6. Will the current leader(s) be involved in the transition? Are you ready to let go of the control?
7. Are there any potential conflicts of interest that need to be addressed during the succession process?
8. How will your succession plan affect employees, customers, vendors and other stakeholders?

9. What steps need to be taken to develop and prepare the next generation of leaders?
10. Are there any legal or financial matters that need to be addressed?
11. How will you transfer your knowledge and expertise to your successor(s)?
12. How will you measure performance and success during and after the succession process?
13. What communication strategies will be utilized to ensure full transparency and minimize pushback to the succession plan?
14. Is your estate sufficiently diversified so that your children who are not active in the business may be treated fairly?
15. Are your key employees comfortable with your plans for business continuation?

You Have Your Preferred Method. Now, What's Your Plan?

Creating a well-defined succession plan is vital for any business owner looking to ensure the stability of their organization. Key components of this plan should include the identification and selection of suitable successors, readiness assessments, and comprehensive development programs to prepare them for leadership roles. Additionally, addressing the legal and financial aspects of the transition, establishing a clear communication strategy, and setting a realistic timeline are all vital.

The role of the current owner post-transition must also be clearly defined, along with having effective contingency and evaluation mechanisms in place. By meticulously planning each of these areas, a business owner not only secures the future of their business but also facilitates a smooth and successful leadership transition that can withstand the tests of time and unforeseen challenges. Keep this information in your back pocket as you move onto the planning process.

In Chapter Six, the centerpiece of our book, we introduce a practical five-step process to develop your succession plan.

CHAPTER 6

The Succession Solution

Now that you know how to set yourself up for success during the planning process, you can confidently start planning your succession.

In this chapter, we will accompany Dr. Samuel Harris, a devoted physician in eastern North Carolina, as he navigates the creation of a succession plan for his medical practice. As we explore Dr. Harris's journey, you may find parallels to your own challenges and transitions in managing a business.

Dr. Harris's practice, deeply integrated into the fabric of his close-knit community, has grown from a single location to multiple offices across three counties over the last forty years, becoming a cornerstone of trust and care. As he approaches a critical transition, the importance of a well-structured succession plan becomes evident, not only to maintain the continuity of care for his community but also to secure his own legacy.

As you journey through Dr. Harris's story, reflect on how his dedication and strategic planning mirror your commitment to your business. This chapter will guide you through the same five-step process that Dr. Harris used, providing you with a blueprint to design your own succession plan that ensures a smooth transition and secures the future of your business.

Historically, the stark reality is that only two out of ten businesses that go on the market will successfully sell. This translates to a disheartening 70-80% of businesses failing to find a buyer when they decide to sell. For family businesses, the outlook is similarly challenging, with only 30% successfully transferring to the second generation, a mere 12% surviving into the third, and an even scarcer 3% enduring to the fourth generation and beyond. These statistics underline a harsh truth: without a solid and actionable succession plan that focuses on making your business presentable, desirable, marketable, and financeable, the likelihood of a business surviving beyond its founder is minimal at best.

Dr. Harris's situation mirrors these challenges. With a beloved practice at stake, the urgency to devise a succession plan could not be greater. The decision looms: how does he ensure that the medical practice not only survives but thrives in the hands of the next generation?

Step 1 – Preparation

Preparation is the first critical step in the succession planning process, setting the stage for a smooth transition. For Dr. Harris, this involves:

Business Assessment: Conducting a thorough assessment of the practice's current operations, financial health, and market position. This includes reviewing patient care standards, operational efficiency, financial performance, and employee satisfaction.

Risk Evaluation: Identifying potential risks that could impact the transition or future operations. This could include market risks, regulatory changes, or internal challenges within the practice.

Advisory Team Assembly: Dr. Harris assembles a team of trusted advisors including a financial planner, a business attorney, a CPA, and perhaps a succession planning consultant. This team will provide expert advice and help navigate the complexities of the succession process.

Defining Goals and Objectives

Setting goals and objectives that are specific, measurable, and achievable within a timeframe is essential for guiding the succession process and ensuring the continued success of the practice.

Dr. Harris focuses on:

Short-term Goals: These include improving certain operational efficiencies, increasing patient satisfaction scores, or updating technology and equipment in the practice.

Long-term Objectives: Dr. Harris outlines his vision for the practice's future, which include expansion plans, diversification of services, and maintaining a certain level of profitability. These objectives help shape the strategic direction of the practice post-transition.

Legacy Considerations: It's important for Dr. Harris to ensure that the practice continues to uphold the values and standards he set. This includes maintaining high-quality patient care and a positive work environment.

Identifying the Right Successor

Choosing a successor is perhaps the most personal and critical decision in the succession planning process. Dr. Harris takes several steps:

Internal Candidates: Initially, Dr. Harris evaluates potential internal candidates, such as family members or current employees who have demonstrated leadership potential and commitment to the practice's culture. In his case, his daughter Anna shows promise.

Assessment of Competencies and Fit: Dr. Harris assesses Anna's decision making and leadership skills, experience, and her alignment with the long-term goals of the practice. This includes evaluating her medical expertise, her understanding of business operations, and her vision for the practice's future.

Developmental Needs: Identifying any gaps in Anna's skills or experience is crucial. Dr. Harris plans targeted training and development opportunities to prepare her for leadership. This might include shadowing him, attending leadership workshops, or getting additional certifications in business management or specialized areas of medicine.

Trial Projects: Dr. Harris will assign Anna specific projects or leadership roles within the practice to gauge her capabilities and readiness for the job. This provides both practical experience and an opportunity for Dr. Harris to see how well she handles responsibility and adversity.

By meticulously addressing each of these areas, Dr. Harris ensures that the foundation of the succession plan is solid, the goals are clearly defined and aligned with his vision, and the successor is well-prepared to lead the practice into the future. This structured approach sets the stage for the practice's continued success and growth under new leadership.

Step 2: Development of the Succession Plan

As Dr. Harris prepares to turn the page to a new chapter in his life, the intricacies of planning give way to decisive action. The journey of succession is like putting together a detailed jigsaw puzzle; every piece must align precisely to ensure the continuity of Dr. Harris's practice and a smooth transfer of ownership.

Creating a Timeline

Dr. Harris, with the strategic guidance of his advisory team, crafts a detailed timeline for the transition. This timeline is the backbone of the succession plan, delineating every critical milestone from the initial training sessions to the final transfer of ownership. It ensures that every phase is timed perfectly to maintain operational flow and mitigate disruptions. Each step is carefully plotted, much like a marker on a navigator's map, guaranteeing that both the minutiae and the major leaps forward are executed according to plan.

Forming the Succession Team

Understanding the magnitude of the task at hand, Dr. Harris assembles a talent-filled Succession Team tailored to the size and complexity of his organization. This team is comprised of experts from various fields: a CPA, Business Attorney, Personal Attorney, CFO, Value Advisor, Financial Advisor, Banker, and a consultant. Each member is selected for their specialized knowledge crucial for covering all facets of the succession process.

Dr. Harris entrusts the consultant with the role of project manager to coordinate this multidisciplinary team, allowing him to remain focused on his medical duties while the transition is managed smoothly. As demonstrated in Dr. Harris's approach, larger, more complex businesses may require a more extensive team with diverse expertise to address intricate governance structures and business processes, whereas smaller businesses might benefit from a more streamlined, tightly knit team that can make decisions quickly and with greater unity.

Developing Successors

Central to the plan is preparing the chosen successor, his daughter Anna, for her future role. Dr. Harris and his team design a comprehensive training program tailored to Anna's needs. This program covers everything from clinical operations to the nuances of business management, ensuring she acquires a holistic understanding of running the practice. The aim is not just to prepare Anna for the role but to equip her to excel, ensuring she can carry on her father's legacy with confidence and pride.

Defining Roles and Responsibilities

As the blueprint becomes more defined, Dr. Harris works to establish clear roles and responsibilities for Anna and other key members within the practice. This clarity is essential to avoid any ambiguity about who is responsible for what. Clear boundaries and expectations are set, creating a new operational structure within the practice that supports a smooth transition and fosters respect and understanding among all team members.

Financial Planning

Next, Dr. Harris tackles the financial considerations of the succession. Alongside his financial advisor, he works with the business broker to assess the practice's valuation, explore various financing options, and plan for future fiscal responsibilities. This stage also includes personal financial planning to ensure that both the practice's and Dr. Harris's financial needs are met during and after the transition.

Legal and Ownership Structure

The legal framework of the transition is crafted with the help of Dr. Harris's CPA and legal team. They determine the most effective way to transfer ownership, adapting existing legal structures to fit the new leadership format. This careful planning ensures all legal requirements are met and that the transition is not only smooth but also secure.

Estate Planning

Finally, estate planning aligns Dr. Harris's personal assets with the professional transition. By integrating his personal estate plans with the business succession strategy, Dr. Harris safeguards his family's financial future and ensures that no conflicts arise from the succession. This alignment is crucial in maintaining harmony both within the family and the business.

Through this detailed and thoughtful planning, Dr. Harris does more than prepare for a transition; he crafts a legacy that is poised to thrive well into the future. This ensures that his practice will continue to serve the community with the same level of dedication and care that has been its hallmark under his stewardship.

Step 3 – Communications and Documentations

Effective Communication

Effective communication is pivotal in managing expectations and securing the support of all parties involved in the succession process. Here's how Dr. Harris ensured comprehensive communication:

Family Meetings: Dr. Harris schedules these meetings at regular intervals, ensuring they are structured and focused. Each meeting starts with updates on the progress of the succession plan and then opens up for discussions on any concerns or suggestions. This fosters an environment where family members feel heard and valued, and any potential conflicts can be addressed promptly and constructively.

Engaging Key Stakeholders: Communication with stakeholders goes beyond mere announcements; it involves strategic engagement to ensure continued support and trust:

Employees: Dr. Harris holds informational sessions with staff to explain how the transition will affect them and the practice. He reassures them about job security and discusses potential changes in roles or procedures.

Patients: Through newsletters and during appointments, patients are informed about the upcoming changes in leadership, underscoring that the quality of care will remain high and possibly even improve.

Suppliers and Business Partners: Personal meetings and official communications are used to assure suppliers and business partners of the practice's stability and continuity under the new leadership.

Community Outreach: Dr. Harris participates in community events and local media interviews to communicate the practice's future plans, enhancing the practice's reputation and community trust.

Meticulous Documentation

To ensure the legality and clarity of the succession process, meticulous documentation is crucial. Here's how Dr. Harris approaches this critical task:

Drafting a Comprehensive Succession Plan: The document outlines the vision for the transition, detailing every aspect from timelines to responsibilities. It serves as a master blueprint that guides all succession-related activities.

Legal Agreements: Important legal documents include:

Shareholder Agreements: A Shareholder Agreement is like a rulebook for the owners of a company. It's a legal document that lays out who owns what, who gets to decide what, and how different situations should be handled within the business. The following is a breakdown of what typically goes into one:

1. *Ownership Details*: It tells you who owns which shares and sets the rules for if and how shareholders can sell or transfer their stakes.

2. *Voting and Decisions*: This part is all about how big decisions are made. It details voting rights and what happens when shareholders don't agree on something.

3. *Profits (Dividends)*: The agreement outlines how profits are shared as dividends among shareholders and when these payments are made.

4. *Management Roles*: This section of the agreement outlines the structure of the company's leadership. It details the process for forming the board of directors (if required) and defines the roles and responsibilities at the executive level. Essentially, it sets the framework for who makes the key business decisions and how those decisions are made, ensuring that the company's management is clearly organized and effective.

5. *Exiting the Business*: There are buy-sell rules, sometimes called buyout provisions, which explain what happens if a shareholder wants to leave the company, or if they pass away or can't perform their duties anymore.

6. *Handling Disputes*: If shareholders have a disagreement, the agreement outlines how to resolve these issues without having to go to court.

7. *Maintaining Ownership Balance*: It includes pre-emptive rights to make sure that existing shareholders have the chance to buy new shares and keep their ownership percentage stable if the company issues more shares.

This agreement is about making sure everyone's on the same page and protecting not just the individual shareholders but also the business itself. It sets up a clear, structured way to handle everything from daily operations to major changes, ensuring the company runs smoothly no matter what comes its way.

Estate Plans: Dr. Harris works with his estate planning attorney to ensure that his personal assets are protected and integrated with the business succession plan. This includes trusts, wills, and directives that are aligned with his succession goals.

Employment Contracts for New Roles: As roles within the practice shift, new contracts are drafted to define the terms of employment for successors and key employees, ensuring clarity and legal compliance.

Buy-Sell Agreements: These are reviewed and revised as necessary to accommodate new ownership structures and provide clear instructions on how shares can be transferred in the event of another succession or exit.

Record Keeping: All meetings, decisions, and changes are recorded meticulously. This includes keeping minutes of all family and stakeholder meetings and updating the succession plan document as decisions are made and strategies evolve.

Through effective communication and meticulous documentation, Dr. Harris not only maintains control over the succession process but also ensures that every stakeholder's interests are considered and safeguarded. This dual approach minimizes misunderstandings and maximizes compliance and support, setting a firm foundation for the future continuity of the practice.

Step 4 – Implementation and Review

As the succession plan for Dr. Harris's medical practice is set into motion, this critical phase, Implementation and Review, ensures that the strategic vision smoothly transitions into actionable steps. This is the real test of the planning's effectiveness, focusing on detailed execution and responsive adjustments.

Implement the Plan

The implementation begins with a structured handover of responsibilities to Anna. This process is carefully staged:

Phased Responsibilities: Tasks and responsibilities are transferred incrementally. Initially, Anna might start with managing a few operational aspects under supervision and gradually take on more strategic roles, such as making key business decisions.

Structured Oversight: Dr. Harris schedules regular check-ins and oversight sessions to guide Anna through complex decisions and provide advice based on his extensive experience.

Feedback Mechanism: An open line of communication is established, allowing Anna to provide feedback on her experiences and any challenges she faces. This helps Dr. Harris understand her development needs and areas where additional support may be necessary.

Monitor Progress

Continuous monitoring is essential to ensure the succession plan remains on track and is effective:

Review Meetings: Regularly scheduled meetings with the succession team are held to assess Anna's progress against the plan's milestones. These meetings help identify any deviations from the expected trajectory and allow for timely interventions.

Performance Metrics: Specific metrics and performance indicators are set up to quantitatively assess the transition's success. These might include patient satisfaction scores, financial metrics, or operational efficiency rates.

Adaptation to Changes: The practice remains agile, ready to adapt the succession plan in response to internal feedback or external changes in the healthcare environment.

Contingency Planning

The unpredictability of real-world scenarios necessitates robust contingency planning:

Emergency Protocols: Dr. Harris and the team develop protocols for potential emergencies that could impact the practice, such as sudden changes in market conditions or personal health issues.

Scenario Planning: Different scenarios are mapped out, and plans are developed for each. This might involve what steps to take if Anna decides she needs more time before taking over certain responsibilities, or if there is a sudden regulatory change affecting the practice.

Succession Safeguards: Safeguards are put in place to ensure the practice's stability is not compromised. This includes setting up legal and financial safeguards that activate in the event of unexpected developments.

By thoroughly implementing the plan, regularly monitoring its progress, and preparing for contingencies, Dr. Harris ensures that the transition not only meets the current needs of the practice but is also robust enough to handle future challenges. This approach increases the odds of a smooth handover and a stable foundation for Anna to lead the practice into its next chapter.

Step 5 – Ensuring Continuity

As we progress into the final phase of Dr. Harris's succession plan, the focus shifts from transition to the enduring success and sustainability of the practice under Anna's leadership. This stage, Ensuring Continuity, is crucial for maintaining the practice's legacy while adapting to new leadership dynamics and the evolving needs of the community.

Conflict Resolution Mechanisms

Effective conflict resolution is essential to maintain harmony and ensure smooth operations during and after the transition. Here's how it was structured:

Predefined Processes: Clear, predefined processes are established to address and resolve disputes efficiently. This includes mediation steps, escalation procedures, and, if necessary, involvement of external arbitrators.

Communication Channels: Open lines of communication are maintained to ensure that issues can be raised and addressed promptly before escalating.

Training: Both Anna and the team receive training in conflict resolution to equip them with the skills needed to handle potential disagreements constructively.

Mentorship and Support

The growth and development of the new leader are critical for the sustained success of the practice. Dr. Harris ensures Anna receives the support she needs:

Ongoing Mentorship: Dr. Harris commits to an ongoing mentorship role, offering guidance and sharing insights from his extensive experience. This mentorship is flexible, adapting to Anna's evolving needs as she grows into her role.

External Coaching: In addition to mentorship from Dr. Harris, Anna can engage with external coaches who specialize in leadership development within the healthcare industry, providing her with a broader perspective and new learning opportunities.

Review and Update the Plan

The business environment is dynamic, and a successful succession plan must be flexible to adapt to changes:

Regular Reviews: The succession plan is reviewed regularly—at least annually—to ensure it aligns with the practice's current operations and future aspirations. These reviews consider internal feedback and external changes in the healthcare landscape.

Adaptive Revisions: Based on the reviews, the plan is revised to address new challenges and opportunities. This might involve redefining roles, adjusting goals, or reshaping strategies to better fit the current context.

This structured approach to ensuring continuity not only solidifies the foundation for Anna's leadership but also instills a culture of proactive adaptation and resilience within the practice. By focusing on these important topics that makeup the Succession Plan, Dr. Harris sets the stage for the practice to thrive!

Next Steps

Succession planning is a complex, time-consuming process, and the complexity of these five steps for success reflects this fact. Take your time digesting the material and reviewing it as you need. Even though this chapter has a lot of relevant information, it's best to work with a professional to complete succession planning thoroughly and in a timely manner.

Up next, we're going to shift our focus to maximizing the value of your business within the next three to five years.

CHAPTER 7

How to Get Top Dollar for Your Business

With a solid succession plan in place, it's time to explore the full potential of what you've built. Whether you decide to pass on the torch or, like Billy Brooks from Arizona, choose to continue leading your thriving business, this chapter is about enhancing your options and securing your future.

Billy, a seasoned second-generation business owner, was struggling with the typical exhaustion from relentless operational demands. I discovered early on that he lacked a succession plan. During our initial discussions, which included a series of Discovery questions, Billy revealed an overly optimistic valuation of his business, a common trait among small to midsize business owners. As an entrepreneur myself, I understand how this can happen. It's easy to become emotionally attached and overly optimistic when you've poured your life into your business.

Billy initially believed his business was worth nearly triple its actual market value. However, upon understanding the true valuation, he decided against selling. Instead, Billy committed to making strategic enhancements and realigning his business vision. Over the following eighteen months, he not only finalized his succession plan but also revitalized his business operations, details of which we'll explore later regarding the steps he took and their significant impact.

As the timing for the planned exit phase approached, I reconnected with Billy to discuss his readiness. To my surprise, he expressed a renewed passion for his business, stating, "Why would I want to sell now? I am having more fun than I have had in years, the company is more profitable than ever, and overall, life is really good." Billy's openness to coaching and his commitment to investing time and resources had not just given him a profitable business, but options for the future that excited him. Those options include:

1. **Option to Sell or Continue:** Billy has the choice to either sell the business now or continue owning and operating it.

2. **Decision Ownership:** With the succession plan document completed, Billy understands that the decision to sell, and its timing, rests solely with him.

3. **Security and Peace of Mind:** The succession plan ensures that Billy and his family are protected in case something unexpected happens to him. This gives him a sense of security, confidence, and peace.

4. **Regular Review:** Billy revisits his options every 90 days.

5. **Preparedness for Opportunities:** Should an unexpected but interested buyer approach, Billy is prepared with an organized Due Diligence file, ready to present and clearly communicate the story and value of his company.

Here's how you can replicate Billy's success and amplify it.

Audit with Fresh Eyes

Conducting a comprehensive audit of every department in a business is crucial, and here's why: when you're deep in the weeds of daily operations, it's all too easy to develop what's called operational myopia. Basically, you're so close to the process that it's hard to spot inefficiencies or redundant procedures that creep in. This is where stepping back and taking a fresh look at each department really makes a difference.

Imagine bringing in external auditors or consultants. These folks come with no preconceived notions about how things should be done in your business, which means they can spot problems you might have missed and point out outdated practices. It's like having a new set of eyes that can see what you can't.

By reviewing each department thoroughly, you're not just tidying up current processes. You're also laying the groundwork for finding innovative ways to boost productivity and improve service delivery. This kind of deep dive helps streamline operations and can lead to some exciting discoveries that propel your business forward.

Manage and Mitigate Risk

De-risking your personal, financial and business life by safeguarding the value of your business is a powerful strategy that will help secure your financial future and protect your company no matter what life throws your way. Business valuations hinge not only on actual performance but also significantly on how risky the business appears from a buyer or successor's perspective. Addressing these risks from personal, financial, and business standpoints can drastically improve both the stability and appeal of your enterprise.

Personal Risks: Life can be unpredictable. Events like death, disability, divorce, accidents, or health issues can abruptly change your capacity to manage your business effectively. Proactively planning for these personal risks is essential. Consider life insurance, disability insurance, and emergency planning to manage your business affairs temporarily or permanently, ensuring continuity and stability.

Financial Risks: Financial vulnerabilities can come from many angles—market fluctuations, personal debts, lawsuits, or even a loss of earnings due to unforeseen circumstances. Protecting yourself involves thorough financial planning, diversifying investments to shield against market volatility, and securing personal assets from business liabilities, possibly through legal structures that separate personal and business finances.

Business Risks: The operational side of your business also carries its own set of risks. These can range from customer concentration, which can lead to revenue issues if a major client leaves, to reliance on key personnel whose sudden departure could disrupt operations. Economic shifts, partner disagreements, safety concerns, data security, compliance issues, and technology failures are additional risks where contingency plans are needed.

For example, to tackle customer concentration risk, diversify your client base to reduce dependency on a few major clients. In addressing risks related to key personnel, develop a strong second line of management through training and empowering your staff. This reduces owner dependence and enhances business continuity. Ensure all your data is secure and that you comply with the latest regulations to avoid legal troubles that can tarnish your company's reputation and financial standing.

Taking proactive steps to mitigate these risks not only secures your business but also boosts its valuation by making it more attractive to potential buyers or successors. They'll see a well-oiled machine that's built to last rather than a risky investment.

By addressing these varied risks, you ensure that your business remains a strong, viable entity that can thrive and adapt, safeguarding your legacy and providing you with peace of mind. This holistic approach to risk management not only enhances your business's resilience but also solidifies its long-term value, making it a safer and more appealing prospect for future transitions.

Incorporate Best Practices

Integrating industry best practices into your business isn't just a good idea, it's essential for keeping your competitive edge razor sharp. Think of this as upgrading your toolkit. This could mean adopting new technologies that speed up processes, enhancing customer service protocols to boost satisfaction, streamlining your supply chain for better efficiency, or updating your safety and compliance measures to meet the latest standards.

By aligning your business practices with those of industry leaders, you're not just keeping up; you're setting yourself up to excel. These leaders have set high standards for a reason as they've found what works best to streamline operations, enhance reputations, and capture larger slices of the market.

When you adopt these best practices, you're doing more than just improving day-to-day operations. You're enhancing your business's reputation, which can attract better partnerships and more customers. You're also increasing your market share and, importantly, boosting your overall business value. It's like giving your business a high-performance tune-up that makes every part of the operation smoother and more effective.

Review and Reduce Client Concentration

Reviewing and reducing client concentration in your business is a critical step if you find that a significant percentage of your revenue depends on just a few clients. Imagine this: you're a potential buyer looking at a business where most of the income relies on one or two clients. That's a big red flag because the stability of your investment could vanish overnight if even one client walks away. That kind of risk can scare off buyers and potentially kill a deal.

So, how can you tackle this issue? As mentioned earlier, you've got to diversify your revenue streams. This might mean enhancing what you already offer—could you add features or improve your service to appeal to a broader audience? Maybe there's room to break into new markets or develop entirely new products that meet untapped customer needs.

In some situations, acquiring a competitor could be a smart move. This can instantly broaden your client base and increase your revenue. But, and it's a big but, this requires thorough due diligence. You need to ensure that this move not only aligns with your overall business strategy but also positively impacts both your top line (revenue) and bottom line (profits).

By taking these steps, you're not just reducing risk; you're building a more resilient and attractive business that can thrive, regardless of the decisions made by any single client.

Perfect Your Due Diligence

Creating a thorough due diligence checklist is like preparing for a major expedition—it's essential for a smooth transition. This checklist is not just a list of tasks; it's a comprehensive guide covering all critical aspects of your business, from financial and legal details to operational and strategic elements.

Think of it as a full health check-up for your company. It helps both you and the successor or potential buyer see the complete picture: what's working well, what needs tweaking, and what might need a major overhaul. This ensures the business is in top shape, with all systems running smoothly, and helps manage potential risks during the transition process.

Successful entrepreneur Mac Lackey, known for his six business exits and as the Founder of ExitDNA, emphasizes the importance of having a current file with your due diligence documents. Whether transitioning the business within your family or to a third party, Mac advises that being able to quickly provide these documents to an interested party creates a perception of an efficient and well-managed operation, adding value to your business.

Additionally, this checklist ensures transparency and boosts the successor's confidence, serving as a detailed map for their journey with fewer surprises. I would recommend setting up an electronic company file on Google Drive or Microsoft OneDrive for due diligence readiness. Though it takes time to set up, it is a crucial step in the succession plan process.

I suggest keeping copies of the following in your Due Diligence file:

- **Corporate Documents** – Articles of Incorporation, Bylaws, Operating Agreements, Shareholder Agreements, Board Meeting Minutes, Stock Certificates and Ledger
- **Financial Records** – Annual Financial Statements (last 3-5 years), Monthly / Quarterly Financial Statements, Tax Returns (last 3-5 years), Accounts Receivable and Payable Aging Reports, Bank Statements (last 1-2 years), Audit Reports
- **Legal Documents** – Contracts and Agreements, Intellectual Property, Litigation History and Legal Correspondence, Insurance Policies, Employment Contracts and Agreements
- **Operational Records** – Business Plan, Marketing & Sales Plans, Product & Service Descriptions, KPI's, Major Vendor and Supplier Lists
- **Employee Information** – Employee Handbook, Org Chart, Employee Contracts & Agreements, Benefits & Compensation Plan, Employee Performance Reviews
- **Compliance & Regulatory** – Licenses, Permits. Compliance Certifications, Environmental Reports, Health & Safety Records
- **Miscellaneous** – Customer Lists & Agreements, Major Correspondence, Market Research, SWOT Analysis

Ensuring that every box is ticked off before and during the transition not only protects your legacy but also sets up the successor for success. This kind of careful preparation makes the whole process a lot less daunting for everyone involved.

Develop Documented Processes and Systems

Implementing documented systems like the Entrepreneurial Operating System (EOS) can be a game-changer for small to medium-sized businesses looking to standardize and streamline operations. Think of EOS as the operating manual for your business—it's there to make sure everything runs smoothly, especially during transitions, which can often be bumpy.

Here's why it's so powerful: documented systems clarify everyone's roles and responsibilities. This isn't just about knowing who does what; it's about ensuring that the business doesn't rely too heavily on any single person, including you, the business owner. With systems like EOS, you ensure that knowledge and processes are embedded in the organization, not just in people's heads. This boosts operational efficiency and keeps the business running smoothly, no matter who's at the helm.

EOS itself is tailored specifically for smaller operations, aiming to boost performance by creating a clear vision, increasing accountability, and enabling data-driven decisions. It helps align everyone with the company's objectives and standardizes core processes to enhance operational consistency and quality. With tools like the Issues Solving Track™ (IDS), it offers effective problem-solving strategies, while also promoting leadership development and a healthier workplace culture.

If you consider EOS for your business, it's crucial to think about your company's size, structure, and specific needs to make sure it's a good fit. Be aware that introducing a new system like this can be met with resistance. Change isn't always easy, and EOS requires rigorous documentation and commitment across the board to truly embed these new practices into your business fabric. To learn more about EOS, visit (https://www.eosworldwide.com)

Invest in Leadership Development

Developing your leadership team and training managers is not just a box to check. It's a crucial strategy to enhance the value of your business in the eyes of potential buyers.

Imagine this: if your business heavily depends on you to operate smoothly, a buyer might see that as a risk. They could worry that once you step away, the whole operation might falter. To mitigate this, buyers will often insist on Non-Compete and Non-Solicitation agreements to keep you from starting a competing business or poaching clients. But there's a more proactive approach.

Instead of the spotlight being solely on you, you'll want to shift it onto your leadership team. This move reassures buyers about the soundness of your business post-exit. The key to this transition? Building out a leadership team that's not only capable of making decisions but properly empowered to do so and can also be effective in leading their teams.

To ensure your leadership team is set up to excel, investing in their training is essential. This isn't just another expense; it's an important investment in your business's future. Proper training can pay off tremendously, leading to higher employee engagement, lower employee turnover rates, and ultimately, increased productivity, and enhanced profitability.

By empowering your leaders and ensuring they are well-trained, you make it a more attractive and valuable proposition for a potential buyer.

Personal and Professional Development

In today's fast-paced business environment, personal and professional development are more than just buzzwords—they're essential ingredients for sustaining a competitive edge and ensuring the long-term vitality of your leadership. As a leader, staying curious and continually looking for ways to evolve personally and professionally not only sets you apart but also drives your company forward.

One effective way to bolster your growth is by joining a peer group such as Vistage. These groups provide a collaborative space where you can share challenges, exchange solutions, gain fresh insights, and build supportive relationships with fellow leaders. The shared experiences within these groups can accelerate your learning and help you navigate the complexities of the business world more effectively.

But personal growth doesn't stop at networking. Expanding your business acumen is crucial, especially in specialized areas like exit planning—a vital process as you prepare to eventually transition out of your business. Resources we recommend include:

- ExitDNA (https://exitdna.com)
- The Exit Planning Institute (https://exit-planning-institute.org)
- XPX - Exit Planning Exchange (https://www.exitplanningexchange.com)
- Always About People (https://alwaysaboutpeople.com)
- L-21 Group (https://www.l-21group.com)

These organizations offer a wealth of knowledge, resources and tools designed to help prepare you for a successful business exit. These platforms can help you understand the best practices and strategies to maximize your business's value and ensure a smooth handover.

Here are five ways these resources can help prepare you for your business exit:

1. **Comprehensive Education:** Dive into various aspects of exit planning through webinars, articles, courses, and certifications offered by platforms like ExitDNA and The Exit Planning Institute. Their educational content covers everything from valuation enhancement and legal considerations to financial planning and market timing.

2. **Expert Guidance:** Learn from the seasoned experiences of industry experts. Their practical advice can

help you navigate the complexities of exit planning, offering reliable strategies that have been tested in the field.

3. **Networking Opportunities:** Connect with other business leaders and professionals engaged in exit planning. These relationships can provide support, fresh perspectives, and even lead to strategic partnerships.

4. **Tools and Templates:** Utilize checklists, templates, and model documents to streamline your exit planning efforts. These tools provide clear guidelines and can be tailored to fit the specific needs of your business.

5. **Continuous Learning and Support:** Stay updated with the latest developments and adjust your strategies accordingly with ongoing support from these resources. This is crucial for adapting to changing market conditions and regulatory landscapes.

Investing in these areas of development will help prepare you for the future and ensure that you lay a strong foundation for your successor. By embracing these resources, you enhance your strategic thinking regarding both long-term business sustainability and your life's next chapter.

Succession Planning Isn't the End of a Journey

Your journey doesn't have to end with a succession plan. It's about continuously creating value and enjoying the fruits of your labor. Let's transform your business into one that flourishes, whether you're steering the ship or not. Start taking decisive action today to shape your business's future with both confidence and clarity. This proactive approach will not only secure your legacy but also empower your team, ensuring that your business thrives in any scenario.

Part of that decisive action is a significant shift from hands-on business owner to coach and mentor. Chapter Eight covers the cornerstones of these shifting roles and how you can personally prepare yourself to navigate this change.

CHAPTER 8

Navigating the Founder Shift

Transitioning leadership within a company, particularly from a founding business owner to a chosen successor, is a profound and multifaceted process. This chapter will explore the significant transformation that occurs when a founder shifts from being the hands-on, day-to-day leader to a mentor and coach.

It's not just about passing the baton; it's about ensuring the successor is fully prepared to take over the reins effectively. You'll discover how this journey involves gradually delegating operational responsibilities, becoming a source of knowledge and guidance, facilitating the successor's learning and development, encouraging independent decision-making, and building a supportive relationship. Additionally, we'll discuss the importance of introducing the successor to key stakeholders, ensuring alignment with company culture, and monitoring the transition plan. By understanding and embracing these changes, you can help secure the long-term stability and success of the company while fostering the next generation of leadership.

Delegating Operational Responsibilities

One of the first changes that occurs is the gradual delegation of operational responsibilities. As the founder, you will begin to transfer the management of day-to-day tasks and decisions to your successor. This involves entrusting them with handling routine operations, team management, and decision-making processes that you previously oversaw. By stepping back from the daily grind, you allow your successor to gain hands-on experience and develop a deeper understanding of the business's inner workings. This shift is essential for your successor to build confidence and competence in their new role while you transition to a more strategic oversight capacity.

Becoming a Source of Knowledge and Guidance

As you step back from day-to-day operations, your primary function will shift to providing knowledge and guidance. This involves sharing your extensive experience and insights with your successor. Your years of experience have given you a deep understanding of the industry, the business's history, and its strategic direction. By openly sharing this knowledge, you help your successor navigate the complexities of the business environment. This mentorship is not just about transferring information but also about helping your successor develop a strategic mindset and critical thinking skills.

Facilitating Learning and Development

A crucial part of your new role is to facilitate the learning and development of your successor. This involves identifying areas where they may need additional training or exposure and providing opportunities for growth. Introduce them to important industry contacts, involve them in high-level strategic meetings, and encourage participation in leadership development programs. By doing so, you ensure that your successor is well-prepared to take on the leadership role and can handle future challenges effectively.

Encouraging Independent Decision-Making

Encouraging your successor to make independent decisions is a pivotal aspect of the transition. You must strike a delicate balance between offering guidance and allowing them to take the initiative and make their own choices. This empowerment is essential for your successor to develop their own leadership style and build credibility within the organization. Your role shifts from being the primary decision-maker to being a coach who provides feedback and support as your successor navigates new challenges and opportunities.

Building a Supportive Relationship

The relationship between you and your successor is foundational to a successful transition. This relationship should evolve into a supportive and collaborative partnership characterized by open communication and mutual respect. Regular check-ins, feedback sessions, and strategic discussions help align expectations and address any concerns. This ongoing dialogue ensures your successor feels supported and confident in their new role while also providing you with insights into the transition process.

Gradually Reducing Involvement

Over time, you will gradually reduce your direct involvement in the company's operations. This phased approach allows your successor to take on increasing levels of responsibility while still having you available for guidance. Eventually, you may transition to an advisory role or serve on the board of directors, providing strategic input without being involved in daily management. This gradual reduction in involvement helps ensure a seamless transition and allows your successor to fully assume their leadership role.

A great exercise at this point is for you, as the business owner, to take a three- or four-week vacation and completely unplug from the business. This creates a win-win opportunity: your successor gets a true sense of what the new role will entail, and you get to enjoy a much-needed break from the daily stress of work. Upon your return, you can debrief with your successor, discuss their experiences, and offer coaching if needed.

Introducing Successor to Key Stakeholders

An important task is introducing your successor to key stakeholders, including clients, suppliers, and business partners. Building these relationships early on helps your successor establish credibility and trust, which are crucial for maintaining business continuity and stability.

You can start by arranging meetings and events where you personally introduce your successor, highlighting their strengths and the reasons you chose them as your successor. This helps stakeholders feel more comfortable and confident in the new leadership. Additionally, involving your successor in critical negotiations and discussions allows them to demonstrate their competence and build rapport.

Another effective strategy is to share your successor's contact information with stakeholders and encourage direct communication. This not only fosters a sense of independence but also enables your successor to form their own connections and understand stakeholder expectations firsthand.

Finally, consider mentoring your successor on the nuances of each key relationship, including historical contexts, preferred communication styles, and any unique preferences stakeholders may have. This insider knowledge can significantly enhance your successor's ability to manage these relationships effectively.

Ensuring Alignment with Company Culture

Ensuring that your successor is aligned with the company's culture and values is critical. Spend time discussing the company's mission, vision, and the unwritten rules that guide everyday operations. This cultural alignment is essential for maintaining the company's identity and ensuring a smooth leadership transition.

Start by sharing stories and examples that illustrate the company's core values in action. This helps your successor understand how these values shape decision-making and behavior within the organization. Encourage them to participate in team building activities and company events to experience the culture firsthand.

Additionally, consider creating a mentorship plan where your successor meets with long-term employees who embody the company's values. These employees can provide valuable insights into the company's cultural nuances and help your successor build strong internal relationships.

Finally, regularly review and discuss how well your successor's actions and decisions align with the company's values. Provide feedback and guidance to help them internalize these principles and apply them consistently in their leadership role.

Monitoring and Adjusting the Transition Plan

The transition plan should be dynamic, with regular monitoring and adjusting as needed. Stay actively involved in evaluating your successor's progress and make necessary changes to address emerging challenges or opportunities. Flexibility in the transition process can help accommodate unforeseen issues and ensure a successful handover.

Schedule regular check-ins to discuss progress, setbacks, and any adjustments needed in the plan. Use these sessions to provide constructive feedback and identify areas where additional support or training might be required. Encourage open communication so your successor feels comfortable sharing their experiences and challenges.

Another important aspect is setting measurable goals and milestones. Track these milestones to gauge the successor's development and the effectiveness of the transition plan. Celebrate achievements to boost morale and reinforce positive behaviors.

Additionally, consider seeking feedback from other stakeholders, such as employees, clients, and partners. Their perspectives can provide valuable insights into the successor's performance and areas needing improvement.

By embracing these changes and additional tasks, you can successfully transition from a hands-on leader to a mentor and coach. This approach not only helps your successor become ready to lead but also gives you time to gradually withdraw and begin to transition to your next chapter of life. As a result, it ensures the long-term stability and success of the company.

Final Steps of Transition

After you've taken time away from work, established connections between your successor and stakeholders, and attended to all the coaching and mentoring you can handle, you'll start to see the finish line. At some point, your transitional phase will come to an end, and you'll officially transfer ownership. But this isn't as simple as signing a document and shaking hands. Chapter Nine will cover the eight critical finishing touches of a successful transition.

CHAPTER 9

Sealing the Deal

Transitioning the ownership of your business is a monumental step that involves much more than just signing on the dotted line. As you prepare to complete this significant transaction, there are eight critical areas you need to address to ensure a smooth and successful transition.

In this chapter, we will delve into each of these areas, providing you with insights and actionable recommendations. Additionally, we will suggest a "personal activity" for each area to help you maximize the benefits and navigate this process with confidence and clarity. Let's embark on this journey to seal the deal and set the stage for a fulfilling new chapter in your life.

Embracing Change and Acknowledging Emotions

As the business owner, it's natural to experience a range of emotions when facing significant changes both personally and within your business. The decision to transition ownership is a monumental step that affects not only the business but also your personal identity and purpose. Acknowledge these emotions openly and give yourself the space to process them. Reflect on your journey—the achievements, the challenges overcome, and the dedication you've invested. This period of transition is a time to honor your hard work and prepare for the future.

Personal Activity

Embracing change involves more than just accepting the inevitable shifts that come with transferring ownership. It's a process of internal alignment where you reconcile your past achievements with future uncertainties. Consider writing a reflective journal where you chronicle your journey, highlighting pivotal moments and lessons learned. Engage in mindfulness practices or seek counseling if the emotional burden feels overwhelming. By doing so, you create a safe space to explore your feelings and prepare mentally for the new chapter ahead.

Communicating with Family

Open communication with your family is essential during this time. They are likely to be affected by the changes as much as you are. Sit down with them and discuss the transition, addressing everyone's expectations and concerns. It's important to ensure that your family understands the reasons behind your decision and the impact it will have on their lives. Be honest about your feelings and listen to theirs. This transparent communication will help align everyone's expectations and foster a supportive family dynamic.

Personal Activity

Effective communication with your family goes beyond a single conversation. It involves ongoing dialogue and check-ins to ensure everyone feels heard and understood. Consider holding regular family meetings where updates are shared, and concerns are addressed. Use tools such as family therapy sessions if needed to navigate complex emotions and maintain harmony. Transparency and empathy are key to ensuring that your family's support system remains strong and united through the transition.

Considering Lifestyle Changes

Transitioning out of your business brings significant lifestyle changes. Prioritize your health and well-being during this time. Consider how your daily routines will change and what steps you need to take to maintain a balanced and healthy lifestyle. This might include adopting new hobbies, spending more time with loved ones, or engaging in activities that promote physical and mental well-being. We will discuss this in much more detail in Chapter 10.

Personal Activity

Proactively design your post-transition life. Create a vision board or list of goals to visualize your new lifestyle. Identify activities that bring you joy, whether it's traveling, volunteering, or learning new skills. Develop a structured routine that includes physical exercise, healthy eating, and mental wellness practices like meditation or yoga. Surround yourself with a supportive community that encourages your new pursuits and helps you stay motivated.

Financial Planning

Work closely with your financial advisor to develop a comprehensive plan that covers your retirement needs, strategies, and estate planning. Ensure that you have a clear and accurate business valuation and are comfortable with the sale terms. Update your estate plan to reflect the changes in your assets and establish an emergency fund to safeguard against unexpected financial challenges.

Personal Activity

Financial planning for your retirement and beyond requires meticulous attention to detail and forward-thinking strategies. Conduct regular reviews with your financial advisor to adjust your plan as needed. Diversify your investment portfolio to minimize risks and maximize returns. Explore tax-efficient strategies to preserve your wealth and consider long-term care insurance to protect against potential health-related expenses. Establish a legacy plan that outlines charitable donations or bequests to causes that matter to you, ensuring your impact extends beyond your lifetime. By taking these steps, you'll create a secure and fulfilling financial future.

Legal and Financial Documentation

Complete all necessary legal and financial documentation to formalize the ownership transition. Inform all stakeholders about the change in ownership, emphasizing continuity and the future direction of the business. Ensure all legal requirements are met for a smooth and transparent transition. The new owner should be well-informed and prepared to take on their role.

Personal Activity

Legal and financial documentation is the backbone of your successful ownership transition. Work with a legal team specializing in business transactions to draft and review all necessary documents, such as buy-sell agreements, transfer of ownership forms, and non-compete clauses. Schedule meetings with key stakeholders, including employees, clients, and suppliers, to communicate the transition plan and address any concerns. Provide comprehensive training and support to the new owner to ensure they are equipped to lead the business effectively. By taking these steps, you'll ensure a smooth and transparent transition for everyone involved.

Supporting the Successor

Ensure your successor has the necessary support systems in place. Provide them with guidance, share your knowledge and experience, and introduce them to key contacts. This support will help maintain the stability and success of the business during the transition period.

Personal Activity

Supporting your successor goes beyond initial guidance. Establish a mentorship program where you offer ongoing advice and feedback. Facilitate introductions to industry networks and key clients to help them build strong relationships. Create a comprehensive transition plan that outlines critical milestones and performance metrics. Encourage your successor to seek continuous learning opportunities, such as leadership courses or industry conferences, to enhance their skills and confidence. By providing this support, you'll help ensure the continued success and stability of the business.

Celebrating the Transition

Organize a formal event to celebrate the transition. This is an opportunity to acknowledge past successes and express optimism for the future of the business under new ownership. Celebrate milestones achieved, thank your team for their hard work, and officially welcome the new owner. This celebration marks the end of one chapter and the beginning of another, filled with new possibilities and opportunities.

Personal Activity

A celebration event serves as a symbolic gesture that honors the past while looking forward to the future. Plan an event that reflects your company's culture and values, incorporating meaningful elements such as speeches, awards, and commemorative presentations. Involve all stakeholders, from employees to long-term clients, to foster a sense of community and continuity. Use this occasion to reinforce the company's vision and mission, ensuring that everyone feels part of the ongoing journey. This celebration will not only acknowledge your hard work and dedication but also set a positive tone for the future under new leadership.

Reflection

Sealing the deal is not just about the business transaction; it's about recognizing the personal, emotional, and financial aspects of this significant life change. By addressing these areas thoughtfully and comprehensively, you can ensure a smooth and successful transition, paving the way for a fulfilling new chapter in your life.

Personal Activity

Reflection is a powerful tool in navigating the complexities of your business transition. I encourage you to take time for introspective activities, such as writing letters to your future self or creating a personal mission statement for your next phase in life. Celebrate your legacy and the impact you've made, while embracing the opportunities that lie ahead. By viewing this transition as a holistic journey, you'll cultivate a sense of closure and excitement for what the future holds. This period of reflection will help you honor your past achievements and prepare mentally and emotionally for the new chapter ahead.

The Deal is Done...What Do You Do Now?

A big congrats to you now that the deal is done! Up until this point, our focus has been on the business transaction; however, an essential part of the succession plan is your personal transition—the next chapter of your life. Once the transaction is complete, where do you go from here?

Studies show that business owners who exit their business without a real plan often feel unfulfilled within a year. How can you make this transition successful, and which resources will accelerate this success?

We will discuss all this and more in the next chapter. Let's explore how to navigate this new phase with purpose and excitement, ensuring your personal journey is as successful as your professional one.

CHAPTER 10

Your 10X Future After the Sale

Congratulations on sealing your business transaction! You're now at the dawn of an exciting new chapter in your life. Some of you are probably feeling extreme relief, while others are anxious and frightened. What's next?

Transitioning from a business owner to a new identity is a significant change. It's not uncommon for many to feel unfulfilled and unhappy by the end of the first year, but don't worry, there are steps you can take to ensure you thrive during this transition.

Initial Reflections

What do you envision for this next chapter of your life? Maybe you see yourself playing golf, traveling, spending more time with family, or volunteering. These are all wonderful ideas, but you might find that doing these activities full-time doesn't always feel fulfilling. It's natural to feel uncertain about how to fill your time meaningfully.

Let me share a story about one of our clients. After selling their real estate business, they moved over 1,200 miles to a retirement community where golf was the main social activity. At first, they were thrilled with the move and the new friendships they were building. However, within six months, the husband felt tired, frustrated, and almost depressed. They weren't enjoying retirement as much as they had expected. This is a common scenario for many who transition without a clear roadmap. Your next chapter of life can be as rewarding and engaging as your career was with the right approach.

Creating Purposeful Meaning

As a successful entrepreneur, your journey doesn't end with selling your business. Begin again by considering what genuinely interests you and what your passions are. Reflect on the activities and fields that energize and excite you. Are there hobbies you've always wanted to explore or skills you wish to develop further? This is the perfect time to dive into those interests.

Next, identify the new opportunities available to you. With your business experience and network, you have a unique set of resources at your disposal. Look for gaps in the market or areas where you can apply your expertise in a new way. Consider mentorship, consulting, or even starting a new venture in a different industry.

Remember, this process might involve some trial and error. Don't be afraid to experiment with different paths. Start small with incremental steps and use each experience as a learning opportunity. Over time, these small steps can lead to significant discoveries about what brings you fulfillment and joy.

Engage with communities related to your interests. Networking with like-minded individuals can open doors to new ideas and collaborations. Additionally, stay open to continuous learning. Enroll in courses, attend workshops, or join professional groups to expand your knowledge and stay inspired.

Ultimately, finding a new purpose is about combining your passions with practical opportunities. By thoughtfully exploring your interests and leveraging your resources, you can create a fulfilling new chapter in your life. This journey not only helps you grow personally but also allows you to contribute positively to others and your community.

Building a Support Network

Feeling uncertain about this new phase? Connecting with others can make all the difference. Reaching out to friends and colleagues who have gone through similar transitions can be incredibly helpful. Socializing more can provide inspiration and guidance, reminding you that you're not alone on this journey.

Deepening relationships during major life changes involves open communication, quality time, and mutual support. Be honest and vulnerable, share your experiences, and show appreciation. Spend time together through shared activities and actively listen to each other.

Reconnect with old friends and join groups with similar interests to expand your support network. Offering and seeking support, expressing gratitude, and being patient are key. Personal growth enhances your ability to maintain strong, meaningful relationships.

Seeking Guidance

Navigating a new life chapter after selling your business can be a daunting task, and seeking third-party guidance offers numerous benefits. Professional advisors, consultants and coaches bring valuable experience and objectivity to the table, helping you to see potential opportunities and pitfalls that you might overlook. They will provide tailored advice based on your unique circumstances, aiding in the development of a comprehensive and realistic plan for your future. Furthermore, third-party guidance often includes access to networks and resources that can be instrumental in successfully transitioning to your next phase of life. Advisors can also help you stay accountable and motivated, ensuring you make consistent progress toward your goals.

Identifying trustworthy third parties to help you create a vision for your next chapter involves several key steps. You want to research potential advisors' backgrounds and credentials, ensuring they have relevant experience and expertise. Next, seek recommendations from peers or other professionals who have undergone similar transitions. It's also beneficial to look for advisors who have a proven track record of success and positive client testimonials. Conduct interviews to gauge their approach and compatibility with your goals and values.

Transparency about their processes and fees is another critical factor in determining their trustworthiness.

The Importance of a Personal Transition Plan

Embarking on this new life chapter can seem overwhelming, but with a well-thought-out plan, it can also be incredibly rewarding. To make this transition successful, create a personal transition plan. I highly recommend you start by discussing your future vision with your spouse and family to outline daily, monthly, and yearly activities. Identify your personal mission, vision, and values for life after the sale.

Gino Wickman's book "Shine" highlights the importance of 10-year thinking, which helps individuals develop a long-term vision, keeping the mind engaged, healthy, and strong. Another valuable resource is The Life Purpose Scan (LPS), which provides insights to help individuals prioritize and customize their plans and support systems. More information on the LPS can be found on the Resources page at the end of this book.

You can take the assessment and receive a personal guided discovery afterwards for $150 by going to https://www.lifepurposescan.com/ legacy.

By taking these steps, you can ensure that your new chapter is filled with purpose, meaning, and joy.

Holistic Wellness

Transitioning to a new chapter in life is a profound journey, and maintaining overall wellness is key to its success. It's essential to take a holistic view of wellness when developing your personal transition plan. Consider five key dimensions: mental & emotional, physical, social, occupational, and financial wellness.

To maintain good health as you age, focus on staying active, eating well, getting enough sleep, and regularly visiting the doctor. For your mental, emotional, and social health, studies show that building a strong social support network, practicing self-compassion, and scheduling regular mindfulness and breathing exercises are beneficial. Men are more than twice as likely as their spouse to struggle with emotional support due to a lack of reliance on others.

By addressing these dimensions and incorporating healthy practices into your daily routine, you can ensure a smooth and fulfilling transition into this new phase of life.

Strategies to Maintain Purpose and Identity

Transitioning to a new life chapter after selling your business can be both exciting and challenging. Maintaining a sense of purpose and identity involves continuous self-reflection and goal setting. Regularly review your personal transition plan with your family and advisors to stay on track.

Engaging in lifelong learning, pursuing hobbies, and getting involved in community organizations can help you find new avenues for personal growth. For instance, you might take up a new hobby like painting, enroll in a cooking class, or volunteer at a local charity.

Transparent communication and patience are key to ensuring you and your spouse are in agreement with the plan. By discussing your goals and progress openly, you can work together to create a fulfilling and purposeful next chapter.

Looking Forward

Struggling to let go of the past? It's time to shift your focus. Dwelling on what you've lost and creating "alternative" versions of past experiences can keep you stuck. You can't change the past, and often, this fixation is tied to fears of losing status and identity. Instead, look forward, practice gratitude, stay open to ways you can learn and grow from others, and get involved.

I would challenge you to think about building on your legacy. Consider writing a blog, biography, memoir, or a book on a topic you are passionate about. Your life, full of ups and downs, holds valuable lessons. Why not share your experiences with the world? Your story will inspire and impact more people than you can ever imagine.

Hats Off to the Future!

As you embark on this exciting new chapter of your life, remember that this transition is a journey of growth, learning, and rediscovery. Embrace the opportunities, build new relationships, explore your passions, and create a fulfilling and purposeful future. Stay open to new experiences, seek support when needed, and continuously reflect on your progress.

By taking these steps, you will not only find joy and satisfaction in your personal life, but also leave a lasting legacy that will inspire others. This chapter of your life holds immense potential—seize it with confidence and enthusiasm. Here's to your 10X future!

CHAPTER 11

The Choice Is Yours

In this final chapter, we review the critical strategies and insights that have been at the heart of "The Family Business Blueprint." Our journey together has highlighted the essential elements for ensuring the longevity and prosperity of your family-owned business. As we conclude, it's time to turn knowledge into action. The strategies and insights provided in this book are only valuable if implemented. Your dedication to ensuring a thriving legacy is commendable.

"Success is not the key to happiness. Happiness is the key to success. If you love what you are doing, you will be successful."
–Albert Schweitzer

Your Roadmap to an Enduring Legacy

Here's your roadmap to ensure your legacy endures and thrives.

Start Now

Begin the succession planning process today. The earlier you start, the more prepared you will be for the transition. Delaying succession planning can leave your business vulnerable to unexpected events such as illness, death, or sudden retirement. Starting now allows you to gradually develop and refine your plan, ensuring all aspects are thoroughly considered. This proactive approach provides you with ample time to identify potential successors, train them, and address any issues that may arise. Early planning also helps in minimizing disruptions to business operations and maintaining stability during the transition period.

Engage Your Family and Stakeholders

Involve your family and key stakeholders in the planning process. Their buy-in and cooperation are vital for a smooth transition. Open communication is essential to ensure everyone understands the plan, their roles, and the expectations placed upon them. This involvement fosters a sense of ownership and commitment to the business's future. Regular family meetings and stakeholder consultations can help address concerns, align goals, and build consensus. Engaging them early on can also uncover valuable insights and perspectives that may enhance the succession plan and ensure it is comprehensive and well-rounded.

Seek Professional Guidance

Don't hesitate to seek help from professionals—whether it's a business consultant, financial advisor, or legal expert. Their expertise can provide invaluable support. Professionals can offer objective insights, identify potential pitfalls, and suggest best practices tailored to your specific situation. A business consultant can help with strategic planning and leadership development, while a financial advisor can assist with wealth management and tax planning. Legal experts can ensure that your succession plan complies with all legal requirements and effectively addresses issues such as estate planning, shareholder agreements, and corporate governance. Utilizing professional guidance can significantly enhance the quality and effectiveness of your succession plan, providing peace of mind and ensuring all aspects are thoroughly addressed.

Use the Succession Solution as Your Blueprint

Implement the step-by-step process outlined in this book to ensure a seamless transition. The Succession Solution is a comprehensive framework designed to cover all critical areas of succession planning.

It begins with assessing the current state of your business and identifying potential successors. Next, it involves developing these successors through training, mentorship, and providing them with gradually increasing responsibilities. The plan also includes detailed financial planning to ensure the business's financial health during and after the transition.

By following the Succession Solution, you create a structured path that addresses leadership development, financial stability, and operational continuity, ensuring that no aspect of the transition is overlooked. This methodical approach minimizes risks and prepares your business to thrive under new leadership.

Maximize the Value of Your Business

Focus on strategies, tools, and resources provided to enhance the value of your business. This includes optimizing operations, improving financial performance, and making the business attractive to potential successors.

Begin by conducting a thorough evaluation of your business processes to identify areas for improvement. Streamline operations to enhance efficiency, reduce costs, and increase profitability. Invest in technology and innovation to stay competitive and improve productivity. Strengthen your financial performance by maintaining healthy cash flow, reducing debt, and increasing revenue streams.

Consider ways to diversify your offerings or enter new markets to enhance growth potential. Additionally, ensure that your business is attractive to successors by building a strong brand, maintaining a positive reputation, and fostering a healthy company culture. These efforts not only increase the value of your business, but also make it a more appealing and viable opportunity for the next generation of leaders.

Regularly Review and Update Your Plan

Succession planning is not a one-time event. Regularly review and update your plan to reflect changes in your business and family dynamics. As your business evolves, so do the circumstances surrounding it. Market conditions, financial performance, and family roles may change, requiring adjustments to your plan. Regular reviews, at least annually, ensure that your succession strategy remains relevant and effective.

Engage in open discussions with family members and key stakeholders to reassess goals, address emerging challenges, and incorporate new opportunities. This ongoing process helps you stay prepared for unforeseen changes and ensures that your succession plan continues to align with your long-term vision.

Commit to Continuous Improvement

Foster a culture of continuous improvement and learning within your business. This will ensure that your successors are always prepared to face new challenges and seize new opportunities.

Encourage your team to constantly seek out new knowledge and skills through ongoing training, workshops, and professional development programs. Implement regular performance reviews to identify areas for improvement and celebrate successes. Promote a feedback-rich environment where employees feel comfortable sharing ideas and suggestions for enhancement.

By continuously refining your processes, adopting best practices, and staying abreast of industry trends, your business can remain agile and resilient. Embracing a mindset of continuous improvement helps create a dynamic and innovative organization that is well-equipped to adapt to change, tackle emerging challenges, and leverage new opportunities. This culture not only strengthens your business but also instills a growth-oriented mindset in your successors, preparing them to lead with confidence and foresight.

By following these steps, you can secure a prosperous future for your business and ensure your legacy lives on. For additional resources and support, see the Resources page at the back of this book and visit our website for online tools available at WhiteWater Consulting.

Closing Thoughts

The journey of succession planning is challenging but immensely rewarding. By taking proactive steps today, you can ensure that your business thrives for generations to come. Your dedication to creating a robust succession plan reflects your commitment to your family's future and the enduring success of your business.

Thank you for allowing me to guide you through this process. As I close, there are two final thoughts to leave you with:

1. Take Action

It would be a shame if you invested all this time reading the book, learning about why succession planning is important, and yet did not take action. Recognize that 7 out of 10 businesses never make it to the second generation, and an even smaller 12 out of 100[5] make it to the third generation due to a lack of planning by the business owner. The ripples of your decision are far-reaching, impacting not just you, but your family, employees, their families, customers, and the communities you are a part of.

2. Secure Your Legacy

It is my hope that by taking the steps outlined in this book, you will have the power to ensure your legacy endures, providing stability and growth for everyone connected to your business. Succession planning is more than just a practical step; it is an act of responsibility and care for the future. It ensures that the dreams, hard work, and dedication you've invested in your business will continue to flourish for generations to come. Make the choice today to secure not only your future but also the future of those you love and who depend on you. The impact of your decision will echo through time, creating a lasting legacy of success and prosperity.

---

[5] SBA

As you move forward, remember that every step you take today shapes the success and stability of your tomorrow.

Note From the Author

We hope you have enjoyed reading this book and found it both informative and inspiring. Our aim has been to serve as a call to action, encouraging you to begin developing your succession plan.

As a family-owned business, your legacy is important, and we are dedicated to being a valuable resource for you. If you have any questions or need further assistance, please do not hesitate to reach out to me at chuck@whitewaterconsulting.net.

Thank you for allowing us to be a part of your journey.

Warmest regards,

Chuck Cooper
Founder, Whitewater Consulting LLC

TOOLS & RESOURCES

Throughout the book we have recommended several tools and resources, and it is our desire to provide you with the links and information you need to access these tools and self–implement based on your needs. If you need additional information, please see the contact information at the bottom of this page.

Books:

Buckets: How Business Leaders Keep Their Hustler's – Kevin Monaghan

Culture By Design (2nd edition) – David J. Friedman

Family Business Playbook: Your Family's Path to Long-Term Success – Pete Walsh Jr. & Richard J. Walsh

In The Company of Family – Melissa Mitchell-Blitch

Leading To The One: Creating Cultures of Clarity Where People Are Engaged, Developed and Fulfilled – Bob Borcherdt and Nicki McLeod

Shine – Gino Wickman

Silence The Imposter: 7 Weapons to Silence Imposter Syndrome – Gary Frey

Start Here: A Guide for Family Business Succession – Sara B. Stern

Straight Talk About Planning Your Succession: A Primer for CEOs – Abby Donnelley

The Seller's Journey – Denise Logan

Traction – Gino Wickman

Unprecedented: Building A Multi-Generational Business on Trust, Respect, and the Valuing of People – Chuck Cooper

Walking To Destiny – Christopher M. Snider

Succession and Exit Planning Groups

ExitDNA: https://exitdna.com

Exit Planning Exchange (XPX): https://www.exitplanningexchange.com

Exit Planning Institute (EPI) & Certified Exit Planning Advisors (CEPA): https://exit-planning-institute.org

Family Business Performance Center: https://familybusinessperformance.com

The Family Business Consulting Group:
https://www.thefbcg.com

Resources for Maximizing Business Growth

Always About People: https://alwaysaboutpeople.com

Bessire & Associates: https://bessire.com

BGW CPA: https://www.trustbgw.com

EOS: https://www.eosworldwide.com

FocusCFO: https://www.focuscfo.com

In2Great: Clarity Based Leadership / The Predictive Index:
https://www.in2great.com

Predictive Index: https://www.predictiveindex.com

SalesXceleration: https://salesxceleration.com

The Metiss Group: https://www.themetissgroup.com

Venn Law Group: https://vennlawgroup.com

WhiteWater Consulting: https://whitewaterconsulting.net

Work Positive: https://www.workpositive.today

Peer Organizations

- C12: https://www.joinc12.com
- EO: https://hub.eonetwork.org
- Vistage: https://www.vistage.com

If you have any questions or require contact information for my trusted connections, please feel free to reach out. You can email me at chuck@whitewaterconsulting.net or call me at 704-236-3131. We have an extensive network across the United States and would be happy to assist you.

ABOUT THE AUTHOR

Chuck Cooper, founder and president of WhiteWater Consulting, is a two-time author whose works have significantly impacted small, midsize, and family-owned businesses. His books, Unprecedented: Building a Multi-Generational Business on Trust, Respect, and the Valuing of People and The Family Business Blueprint: Creating Your Succession Roadmap, offer invaluable insights and practical strategies for maximizing company value, ensuring long-term success, and facilitating smooth transitions in family-owned enterprises.

With a career as an entrepreneur, Chuck is dedicated to enhancing the performance and longevity of businesses. He is passionate about serving current business owners and helping the next generation become the leaders of today. Through his books, consulting work, and speaking engagements, he continues to inspire and guide leaders and organizations throughout the United States.

Chuck has been married to his wife, Debbie, for 39 years, and they have three grown children and eight grandchildren. Outside of work, he mentors and coaches entrepreneurs and serves on the boards of faith-based non-profits in Charlotte. He and his wife love to travel, experiencing new cultures and meeting people from all walks of life.

If you would like to connect with Chuck or learn more about him, you are welcome to visit his websites which are WhiteWater Consulting and ChuckCooper.info